Penguin Handbooks
Cooking for a Baby

Sylvia Hull was born in Newcastle-upon-Tyne and spent the
early years of her life there. After attending Durham University
she settled in London where she has lived, except for a period
in Manchester, ever since.

Growing up in an area with a tradition of good food, and
having a mother in the hotel business, she always enjoyed
creating and experimenting with dishes for all tastes. Her
particular interest in feeding babies, however, began with her
own two children, both fussy and faddish eaters more
interested in the sweet than the savoury. Faced with the
problem of feeding them meals that were nutritionally sound
and still acceptable to their young tastes, she began to devise
her own recipes. Though the results were often 'unconventional
concoctions', they proved the only solution.

Sylvia Hull was editor of the magazine *Mother & Baby* for
ten years. To meet the requests for ideas and recipes which
constantly poured in from desperate mothers, she developed,
with the help and advice of nutritional and medical experts,
the recipes in this book.

She is now a publisher of medical books. Sylvia Hull is
married to the *Daily Mail* cartoonist JON, and they live by
the Thames at Richmond where they grow most of the herbs
for the creative cooking they both enjoy.

Sylvia Hull

Cooking for a Baby

Penguin Books

Penguin Books Ltd, Harmondsworth, Middlesex, England
Viking Penguin Inc., 40 West 23rd Street, New York, New York 10010, U.S.A.
Penguin Books Australia Ltd, Ringwood, Victoria, Australia
Penguin Books Canada Ltd, 2801 John Street, Markham, Ontario, Canada L3R 1B4
Penguin Books (N.Z.) Ltd, 182–190 Wairau Road, Auckland 10, New Zealand

First published by Mother & Baby,
The Illustrated Publications Co. Ltd, 1976
Published in Penguin Books 1979
Reprinted 1981, 1982, 1983, 1984, 1985, 1987

Made and printed in Great Britain by
Richard Clay Ltd, Bungay, Suffolk
Set in Monotype Ehrhardt

Contents

Foreword

There seems at times to be a conspiracy among paediatricians, nutritionists and journalists to make infant feeding into a difficult business replete with threats of health hazards both now and in the future. Mothers may therefore be forgiven if the process of preparing food, and their children's consumption of it, has become something of a nightmare of guilt and anxiety rather than a mutually satisfying exercise. Nevertheless there is now an increasing number of mothers who are re-discovering the interest, pleasure and economy which derive from the personal and intimate provision of food for their children. In doing so they need sensible guide-lines which take into account modern knowledge of the nutritional needs of young children as well as the practical aspects of marketing, preparation, cooking and serving.

I cannot vouch personally for the culinary details in this book because egg-boiling is the ultimate in my own cooking skills. But I have been assured that all the recipes have been tried by cooks and approved by young consumers. If these assumptions are correct, I am convinced that many mothers and babies will be indebted to Ms Hull for providing them with the means to restore some of the joy of eating, and the warmth of human relationships to baby feeding. In addition the meals will be nutritionally excellent and I hope not as expensive as those taken from cans or jars. It is also true that many fathers these days are competent cooks and they will also gain from these instructions on how to feed the youngest members of the family.

Thomas E. Oppé
Professor of Paediatrics
St Mary's Hospital Medical School (London)
July 1976

Introduction

When my first baby was ready and willing to progress to foods other than milk, I was concerned that the baby cereals and other commercially prepared foods recommended were all so fattening, but too unsure of a baby's needs to make my own. Helpful advice was hard to come by, but gradually I acquired enough confidence to prepare meals for her myself.

It became clear that this was a very common dilemma of first-time mothers when, subsequently, as editor of *Mother & Baby* for ten years, I received a constant flow of requests for advice, guidance, ideas and recipes. That is why I wrote this book.

It caters for babies from about four months, when first purées are offered. By about eighteen months of age, if not earlier, most babies will be eating more or less what the rest of the family is having, provided meal times coincide. From nutritional and other experts I have learnt a great deal – not least that cooking for a baby is mostly a matter of common sense. There are very few rules.

I am particularly grateful to the nutritionist, Dr Sally Parsonage, who wrote the excellent 'Feeding Guide' that follows and vetted all the recipes. Special thanks also go to Professor Ronald Illingworth and Nurse Joan Neilson for invaluable comments and advice; and last, but far from least, to four-month-old Kelly and eight-month-old Frances, who cooperatively devoured all the tested recipes offered with unbelievable relish.

To use the book to the best advantage, read the 'Feeding

Guide' and 'Guide to Recipes' first. Whether or not you have vegetarian inclinations, do look at the 'Meatless Baby Fare' too – it is economical as well as nutritious. I very much hope that you will derive immense pleasure, as well as satisfaction from the book, and that your offerings will be consumed with zestful enjoyment.

To avoid bias in the current anti-discriminatory climate, references to babies are sometimes in the masculine and some-times in the feminine. So to all babies – boys and girls – *bon appétit*!

Feeding Guide

by Sally Parsonage, BSc, PhD

Feeding a baby probably causes mothers more worry and anxiety than any other aspect of baby care. The very fact that the vast majority of babies grow into fit and healthy children shows that not much goes wrong with their diet, but of course that is small comfort for a mother whose baby is just starting solid foods.

Fortunately, it is not necessary to become a nutrition expert to ensure that your baby gets a balanced diet, but when you begin to wean your baby, simple guide-lines do help with the inevitable problems that crop up.

Which foods?

Everyday foods can be divided into five main groups, as shown in the chart on page 13. If a baby who is well on to solid food has at least one item from each group every day, you can be pretty certain that he is getting all the nutrients he needs for growth and health. And the more you can vary which food you choose from each group, the better his diet will be nutritionally.

Using this simple guide will ensure that your baby gets a well-balanced diet – without you having to worry about adding up grams of proteins or milligrams of Vitamin C. And it is also easy to substitute foods which are as good nutritionally as the ones baby dislikes or you do not want to give him. For example, if your family is vegetarian, you can replace meat by dairy products, cereals, nuts, peas and beans, as well as using soya flour and soya protein meat alternatives, since all contain protein.

How much is enough?

It is one thing to know *which* foods your baby should eat, but quite another to know *how much* he should have. We are continually being told that as a nation we overeat, but none of us wants to underfeed a baby. It is impossible to say exactly how much food any one baby needs, because, like adults, they vary enormously in their requirements. In fact, it is not unusual to find two babies of the same age and size, and growing at the same rate, but one eating almost twice as much as the other. And, like us, babies have hungry days and not-so-hungry days, which can mislead you into thinking that they are either grossly over-eating or half-starved!

The food group chart gives you some idea of what quantities of foods are needed to provide a baby of about a year old with important amounts of essential nutrients like protein, vitamins and minerals. And of course all these foods also provide baby with calories for energy.

Compared with adults, babies need a surprisingly high calorie intake – for example, if a 10 stone adult needs 2,200 calories a day, you would expect a 14 lb (1 stone) baby to need only 220 calories a day, whereas in fact he needs nearer to 800 calories! Fortunately, most babies are quite good at eating just the right amounts for their individual needs, whether these are more or less than the recommended amounts.

Food groups

(Include something from each group every day)

Group	Foods	Approx. daily portion for a one-year-old baby on a mixed diet	Points to note
I	Meat, poultry, offal (liver, kidney, etc.), white and fatty fish (herring, sardines, etc.), eggs	2 oz meat, offal or fish *or* 1 egg	Serve liver or kidney once a week, and fatty fish and eggs occasionally to improve balance of diet
II	Milk, cheese, yogurt and other milk products	1 pint milk *or* 1 oz cheese and 1 carton yogurt	Vegetarians should have more of these foods
III	Cereals, bread, pulses (peas, beans, lentils, etc.), soya products, nuts	2 oz bread *or* 3 oz peas or beans *or* 2 oz nuts, finely milled	Also an important group for vegetarians – especially soya bean products
IV	Butter, margarine, cooking fats and oils	½ oz butter or margarine	Margarine is slightly better nutritionally
V	Fruit and vegetables	½ fresh orange *or* 1 oz blackcurrants puréed *or* 2 oz green vegetables	Serve both cooked and raw fruit and vegetables daily

Calorie needs

As a guide, here are the average calorie needs of babies and, for comparison, the calorie needs of adults.

Age	Daily calories	Adults	Daily calories
0–3 mths	550	women	2,200
3–6 mths	760	men	2,700
6–9 mths	910		
9–12 mths	1,000		
1–2 yrs	1,200		
2–3 yrs	1,400		
3–5 yrs	1,600		

To help you translate calories into different quantities of various foods which would go to make up a daily diet, the daily calorie needs of a one-to-two-year-old baby are shown below as a day's food intake (one of many possible daily menus).

	Calories
1 pint milk	360
1 oz breakfast cereal	100
1 egg	80
2 oz meat in gravy	150
2 oz peas	30
2 oz boiled potato	50
4 oz stewed apple	40
2 oz egg custard	60
2 oz bread	140
½ oz butter or margarine	110
2 oz cottage cheese	60
½ orange	20
	1,200

A younger baby of, say, six to nine months old, would probably have 1½ pints of milk a day but only half the quantities of the solid foods, making a total of around 900 calories a day. But do remember that these quantities are only a very rough guide, and it is more than likely that *your* baby eats either more or less than these amounts. As long as he is not obviously obese, is growing well and is normally active, you have no cause for worry.

The example of a day's food intake given opposite is also a nutritionally balanced diet – simply because it includes something from each food group on the chart.

Starting solids – when and what?

As with everything else, babies vary enormously in when they will start to accept solid food. But you should generally think in terms of a milk-only diet until your baby is at least four months old, and there is no real need for solids until five or six months. Don't expect your baby to switch from milk only to roast beef and two veg in a few days – the change to a mixed diet will be gradual over a few months, and even then a pint of milk a day is a vital part of a baby's diet.

Start by offering a little puréed vegetable, fruit, or meat stock (see 'Simple Soups') or cereal on the tip of a small clean teaspoon. The best time is after the normal midday milk feed, when you are both relaxed and have plenty of time. Don't be upset if he appears to think the whole idea of solid food is a big con trick – leave it for a few days before trying again, perhaps with a different food. Once he starts taking tiny tastes of solids he will quickly learn to enjoy the little 'extras' after milk feeds.

Beyond first tastes

When your baby is accustomed to taking solid food from a tea-spoon, you can begin to think in terms of replacing some of his daily milk intake by other foods. Milk, whether human, artificial or cow's, is a poor source of iron, and by the time he is five or six months old a baby's store of iron, laid down before birth, is almost used up, so it is important to give him iron-containing foods like meat, offal, soups, egg yolk, cereals, fruit and vege-tables.

All these foods, as you will see from the 'Purées Galore' and 'Simple Soups' sections, are easily prepared by puréeing, sieving, mashing or blending into a consistency suitable for eating without the help of teeth, and of course they also contain other valuable nutrients needed by a growing baby.

Introduce new foods one at a time to avoid confusing or frightening your baby with too many new experiences all at once.

The 'one new food at a time' rule is also important in detecting food allergies which sometimes occur in babies under a year old. Egg white and wheat flour are two foods which may cause allergic reactions, and you may prefer to avoid them completely until baby is older, giving him egg yolk and using baby rice in-stead. But many foods can upset a baby, and it will be easier to trace them if only one new food is given at a time.

Babies vary enormously in the speed at which they change from a milk-only diet to milk-plus-solids, and then to a mixed diet, but the following table gives you a rough guide to the different stages of weaning. If your baby does not conform to this, don't worry – he will progress in his own good time!

Weaning guide

0–4 mths   Milk-only diet, either breast or bottle, plus vitamin drops from one month old as directed by clinic.

4–6 mths   Milk is still major part of diet with vitamin drops. Introduce solids by offering small tastes on a teaspoon after a milk feed. If they are refused at first, try again after a few days. Keep to one new food at a time.

6–8 mths   Time to experiment with different tastes and textures, but iron-containing foods important (see 'Beyond First Tastes', above, for suggestions). Solids can start to replace milk feeds, and baby may enjoy chewing finger foods. He will need more to drink – water, fresh fruit juice or well-diluted fruit drinks. Continue vitamin drops.

8–12 mths   Solid food becomes major part of diet, but baby still needs at least one pint of milk a day (either artificial, breast or cow's).

1 year   Baby can now join in with most family meals, but
onwards   still avoid too much salt, sugar or fats. Still needs one pint of milk a day. A wide variety of foods will ensure a well-balanced diet.

New textures as well as new tastes are an important part of a baby's experience of food. At first, he will probably object to lumpy foods, but suddenly, around six or seven months, he will enjoy chewing, even before he has many teeth.

When he starts to put things in his mouth, around six or seven months, is an ideal time to introduce finger foods which baby can hold himself and chew – pieces of raw apple or pear, or sticks of cooked carrot and celery, as well as the traditional rusks, are suitable. Chewing will help baby to have healthy gums and teeth and can also be a great comfort during teething times. But do not be tempted to give him anything sugary to chew, as sugar which stays in the mouth for any length of time spells ruin for teeth, even before they are through the gums.

Don't forget to give your baby plenty to drink when he starts to eat more solid food, because he will get thirstier than he did on milk alone. Try to avoid sugar-containing soft drinks and squashes as much as possible, particularly between meals – plain water or well-diluted fresh fruit juice is preferable.

A fully mixed diet

By the time he is eight to twelve months old your baby will probably be well on the way to three meals a day, all of them including solid food. He will be used to a fairly wide variety of tastes and textures and be able to share most family meals.

Don't add salt or sugar to baby's food – it might seem dreadfully tasteless to you, but babies prefer blander flavours, quite apart from the fact that both salt and sugar are harmful. Too much salt cannot be dealt with properly by a baby's kidneys, and causes dehydration which can be serious. Sugar is simply extra calories with no nutritive value whatsoever, and plays a large part in tooth decay and, in later life, heart disease.

Excesses of fats should be avoided too because they are also very rich in calories and tend to make meals less easily digestible, but more important, animal fats, such as butter, cream, lard and meat fats, are strongly implicated in heart disease. All this talk of heart disease in adult life may seem very remote to you now, but scientists are just beginning to realize that diet in the first few years of life has an enormous effect on health in later years.

This does not mean that you always have to prepare two

different meals, one for the family and one for the baby, as the rest of the family will also benefit from avoiding too much sugar or fat in their everyday diet. (See 'Adapting Family Meals for a Baby' at the end of this book.)

Other foods which are often not suitable for younger babies include acid-tasting fruits like grapefruit, seed-containing fruits like blackberries, and highly spiced foods like curries. But there are doubtless many babies who have happily consumed un-sweetened grapefruit juice or garlic sausage from an early age without any ill-effects, so it is impossible to make hard and fast rules – your own judgement and your baby's taste is the best guide.

You will find that your baby will naturally enjoy sweet foods like bananas and other fruits, and vegetables such as carrots which are far better for him than sticky sweets, cakes and biscuits. But don't be too puritanical about this – there is no reason why he should not have a little of these as special occasion 'treats'.

Remember that even when baby is on a fully mixed diet for all his meals, he should still have at least one pint of milk every day – if he won't drink milk on its own, give him yogurt and cheese as well as using milk in cooking.

Extra vitamins

Milk is a marvellous food for babies, but it does not contain enough of all the nutrients needed by a quickly growing body. Artificial milks are all fortified with the missing nutrients, but it is still necessary to give babies vitamin drops containing Vitamins A, C and D every day. These can be bought very cheaply from your local welfare clinic, and are easy to give baby on a teaspoon alone or with a little boiled water. As baby progresses to a mixed diet he will get most of the nutrients he needs from his foods, but to make quite sure that his special requirements are met during the critical early years, it is advisable to continue giving the vitamin drops at least for the first year and probably until he is two. Never give your baby more than the stated dose of vitamin drops – too much can be as harmful as too little, so if in doubt, check with your clinic or health visitor.

Food is fun

Most babies love to feed themselves, and, even though the first attempts tend to be somewhat inaccurate, you should encourage your baby to do so. Soon after you have started to feed solids, baby will probably try to grab the spoon and that is the time to give him a spoon to hold while you feed him. Babies learn by copying and he will soon discover how to convey food from the plate into his mouth. It is only a small step from this to being able to feed himself completely, provided the food comes in small pieces that are easy to pick up with his fingers or 'catch' in a spoon.

From the very early days right through childhood your attitude towards food and meal times is vital – if you can stay relaxed you will avoid many upsetting battles. Never force your baby to 'eat up everything' when he has indicated that he does not want any more. Excess food can only do harm by causing overweight with all its problems, and your baby's health is far more important than the waste of a few mouthfuls of food. Humans need food for emotional reasons as well as for nutritional ones, and that goes for babies as well as for adults, so if you can enjoy your meals together as well as giving your baby a balanced and varied diet, you will encounter few problems.

Avoiding fatness

A fat baby is not healthy, and is far more prone to all sorts of illness and disease. If you are uncertain whether your baby is overweight, consult your health visitor or doctor who will advise you if any action is necessary.

Obviously a baby cannot go on the same sort of slimming diet as you would, because he is still growing and developing. So you must cut out unnecessary calories without reducing the nutritional value of his food. To do this, concentrate on foods rich in protein, vitamins and minerals – Groups I, II and V in the chart on page 13 – and cut down on cereal foods (Group III) and fats (Group IV), but without excluding them completely. Protein-rich foods are particularly important because as well as providing the materials for growth they will also satisfy baby's appetite for longer than carbohydrate foods like sugar and starch. Preparing your baby's food yourself has the great advantage that you can control the sugar, cereal and so on that goes into it.

Don't expect baby to lose weight dramatically – in fact, if he does, you are reducing his food intake too strictly. If you can keep his weight steady for a while, excess fat will go as he grows.

But it is much, much better to prevent overweight. Weaning onto a fully mixed diet is a crucial time for establishing good eating habits for life, and this is what these recipes aim to do.

Guide to Recipes

Terms used

Baby cereal : refers to any of the commercially produced fortified baby cereals like Farex, and those by Robinsons. But, for babies under about eight months, baby rice is particularly recommended as it contains no wheat, which some young babies are allergic to.

Baby milk : means whatever liquid milk your baby is having. Cow's milk straight from the milkman's bottle can be used in cooking for babies over five months if it is diluted with an equal amount of water, i.e. half milk to half water. No dilution with water is necessary for babies over eight months.

Breadcrumbs : made in a liquidizer, or grated, from a loaf a day or two old.

Minced meat : butchers' ready-minced beef can be used in recipes specifying minced beef, provided it is prepared in a non-stick frying pan as suggested in the recipe for Minced Beef Casserole on page 120.

Simmer : boil gently covered with a lid.

Steam : as an alternative to baking. To cook in a covered casserole, in the top of a steamer; in an adjustable fan-like steamer basket; or standing in a pan with simmering water half-way up the casserole.

Stock : this always refers to stock prepared as in 'Small Stocks' on page 64, or Baby Soup Stock on page 116. (Ordinary stock and stock cubes are too salty for young babies, water is better.)

Measurements

Ingredients are given in simple British Standard measurements: tablespoons, teaspoons and so on (rounded unless otherwise stated), or in imperial measurements followed by the approximate metric equivalent, e.g. 2 oz (50 g) or ½ pint (250 ml). Oven temperatures are given in Fahrenheit (F), followed by Celsius, which is the same as Centigrade (C), and the appropriate gas number, e.g. 350°F (180°C), Gas 4.

As a check and an aid in multiplying recipes for larger appetites, more than one baby, or for quantities for freezing, here are the conversions used.

Weight		Liquid	
½ oz	12 g	1 fl oz	25 ml
1 oz	25 g	2 fl oz	50 ml
4 oz	100 g	8 fl oz	200 ml
8 oz	225 g	10 fl oz/½ pint	250 ml
12 oz	350 g	¾ pint	375 ml
1 lb	500 g	1 pint	500 ml
2 lb	1 kg	2 pints	1 litre

Oven Temperature			Distance	
°F	°C	Gas		
225	110	¼	½ inch	1 cm
250	120	½	1 inch	3 cm
275	140	1	2 inches	6 cm
300	150	2	3 inches	8 cm
325	160	3		
350	180	4		
375	190	5		
400	200	6		
425	220	7		
450	230	8		
475	240	9		

How much equipment is necessary?

It's up to you – a fork will do many things, but some other items are worth considering. Here are the advantages of a few – take your choice.

Small heavy pan with well-fitting lid: this facilitates simmering with very little water and therefore a minimum loss of nutrition and heat.

Small casserole(s): very useful for baking and steaming in many recipes (though a heatproof cup would do). Buy one with a lid if possible, in Pyrex, earthenware, or other heatproof material, deep rather than wide if you intend to steam with the casserole standing in a pan of simmering water.

Hand blender: excellent for puréeing small quantities of all kinds of foods and a minimum of food is wasted. Specially recommended are the Baby Mouli and the Mothercare Food Blender.

Small sieve with fine mesh: very useful for puréeing many foods, but particularly things like tomatoes and blackcurrants, where seeds and skins have to be discarded for young babies.

Grater: good for cheese and – later – onion which has to be finely chopped.

Measuring jug, tablespoon, dessertspoon and teaspoon: useful to avoid guesswork.

Scales: likewise useful to avoid guessing.

Steamer or steaming basket: very good for gentle cooking of foods like fish, liver and so on, and for small casseroles that would otherwise go in the oven.

Double saucepan: helpful for slow cooking of custards, Welsh rarebits and so on; for defrosting frozen foods; for keeping food hot for short periods; and for saving heat by double cooking.

Heatproof plates: useful for steaming a baby meal (between two plates) over a pan in which something is already cooking.

Electric liquidizer: excellent for many liquid baby dishes, but a bit wasteful for making thickish purées in small quantities as it can be difficult to scrape food off the blades and out of the crevices.

Electric chopper: will mince your own fresh, fat-trimmed meat to a pulp in a flash, very good for pâtés too. Moulinex make one, combined with an electric liquidizer.

Easy-to-clean tray or large bowl and boilable linen or similar towel: keeps all baby cooking and eating equipment hygienically together, covered, after washing, away from equipment used for the rest of the family (only normally necessary up to seven or eight months).

Equipment hygiene

All equipment used for preparing, cooking and serving food for young babies should be very thoroughly washed – all particles of food scrubbed from meshes of blenders, sieves and so on – rinsed and dried.

Up to six to eight months of age it might also be advisable to sterilize any items in glassware like Pyrex, pottery, plastic and so on, as for feeding bottles, by the Milton or a similar chemical method. This chemical method is not suitable for metal items, which can be sterilized by boiling instead, if necessary. As long as equipment can be thoroughly cleaned, however, there is not the same necessity for sterilizing as there is with baby bottles with narrow necks.

Abbreviations

tbsp	tablespoon	rounded
dessertsp	dessertspoon	unless otherwise
teasp	teaspoon	stated
oz	ounce	
lb	pound	
g	gramme	
kg	kilogramme	
ml	millilitre	
fl oz	fluid ounce	
min	minute	
hr	hour	
mth	month	

Recipes

Purées Galore

This is how to prepare food for first tastes – from about four months. Begin with one food at a time and if it goes down well, include it in your baby's diet regularly. Then once she is used to a number of foods, progress to the recipes that follow, many of which incorporate the basic purées.

Quantities given are the minimum practical for one baby, but until she is happily taking teaspoonfuls surpluses are inevitable. Suggestions for using these up are given at the end of the section.

Vegetable Purées

Aubergine or Egg Plant

1 medium aubergine

Wash, slice diagonally, remove seeds and put into about 1 inch (3 cm) boiling water. Simmer, covered, 10–15 mins. Drain. Press through a sieve, discarding the skin and some of the thin liquid that runs through first.

Beetroot

1 small beetroot

If not already cooked, clean well without breaking the skin. Cut stalk to about 2 inches (6 cm) but leave root on. Put in boiling water to cover and simmer with lid on until cooked, 1–1½ hrs (or cook in a pressure cooker for 10–15 mins). If skin comes off easily when pinched, it is done. Remove skin.

Mash with a fork until smooth. (Beetroot may show up red in a baby's bowel movement, but it is harmless.)

Broad Beans

2 pods or 6–8 broad beans

Shell beans. Bring about 1 inch (3 cm) water to the boil in a small pan, add beans and cook covered until tender, 20–30 mins. Drain, saving liquid.

Mash with a fork or sieve, discarding any tough skins. Or put through a hand blender. Mix with a little cooking liquid or baby milk if too thick.

Broccoli

2 or 3 sprigs broccoli

Wash well. Bring about 1 inch (3 cm) water to the boil. Add broccoli and simmer, covered, until cooked, about 15 mins – a fork will slide easily into the stalk part when done. Drain, saving the liquid. Mash with a fork until smooth or put through a hand blender. Add a little cooking liquid or baby milk if too thick.

Butter Beans

2 tbsps butter beans

Soak overnight and pour away soak water. Bring to the boil, well covered with water, and simmer, covered, until soft, about 45 to 60 mins. Drain, saving liquid.

Mash with a fork, or sieve, discarding any tough skin. Or put through a hand blender. Mix with cooking liquid or baby milk – about 1 tbsp cooked beans to ½ tbsp liquid.

Cabbage

2–3 leaves green or white cabbage

Wash leaves, shred and put into 1 inch (3 cm) boiling water. Simmer, covered, until cooked, 10–15 mins – a fork will slide easily into the stalk parts when it is done. Drain and put through a hand blender.

Carrot

1 medium carrot

Scrub well or peel finely. Slice and put into 1 inch (3 cm) boiling water. Simmer, covered, until cooked, 10–15 mins. Drain and mash with a fork.

Cauliflower

2 or 3 sprigs cauliflower

Prepare, cook and purée as for broccoli.

Celery

2 or 3 stalks of celery

Wash, remove root end and leaves. Chop and put into 1 inch (3 cm) boiling water. Simmer, covered, until tender, 15–20 mins. Drain and put through a hand blender.

Courgette

1 small courgette

Wash and trim off coarse stalk and any blemishes. Slice, put into 1 inch (3 cm) boiling water and simmer, covered, until tender, about 15 mins. Drain, saving the liquid. Put through a hand blender, or mash with a fork, adding a little of the cooking liquid for a runnier purée.

Cucumber

a 2-inch (6 cm) piece cucumber

Wash, peel and cut in half lengthways. Scrape away seeds and grate cucumber finely. Mash with a fork.

French or Runner Beans

4 pods French or runner beans, fresh or frozen

If fresh, wash beans, top and tail and remove any stringy bits. Slice diagonally. Put beans into 1 inch (3 cm) boiling water and simmer, covered, until tender, 10–20 mins. (Follow pack instructions for frozen beans.) Drain, saving liquid. Put through a hand blender. Add a little cooking liquid or baby milk if too thick.

Haricot Beans

2 tbsps haricot beans

Soak beans overnight and pour away soak water. Bring to the boil, well covered with water, and simmer with lid on until tender, about 50 mins. Drain and save liquid. Put through a hand blender and mix with a little cooking liquid or baby milk until smooth.

Lentils

2 tbsps lentils   7 tbsps water

Wash lentils in a sieve under running cold water. Bring to the boil in the water and simmer, covered, until soft, 30–40 mins.

Pass through a sieve and add a little baby milk or water if too thick.

Marrow

1 thick slice vegetable marrow

Peel, remove seeds and pith, and cut marrow into cubes. Put into 1 inch (3 cm) boiling water and simmer, covered, until tender, about 10 mins. Drain and mash with a fork.

Parsnip

1 small parsnip

Scrub and peel parsnip. Slice or dice and put into about 1 inch (3 cm) boiling water. Simmer, covered, until tender, 15–30 mins. Mash with a fork.

Peas

4 tbsps peas, fresh or frozen

Bring 1 inch (3 cm) water to the boil and simmer peas in this, covered, 7–10 mins for fresh peas, less for frozen peas. Drain, saving liquid. Press through a sieve or put through a hand blender, adding a little cooking liquid or baby milk if too thick.

Potato

1 medium potato

Scrub clean, remove any blemishes and cook in a pan covered with boiling water and a lid and simmer until tender, 20–30 mins, or bake at 400°F (200°C), Gas 6, until tender, about 45 mins. Peel after cooking and mash finely, adding a little baby milk or water if too thick.

Spinach

4 or 5 leaves fresh spinach or 2–3 oz (75 g) frozen spinach

Wash fresh spinach in a bowl of water, lifting out carefully to allow any grit to sink. Remove any coarse stalks and cut remaining stalks into 1-inch (3 cm) lengths. In ½ inch (1–2 cm) water bring slowly to the boil, covered, and simmer until tender, 10–15 mins. For frozen spinach follow directions on pack. Drain well, and put spinach through a hand blender.

Split Peas

2 tbsps split peas

Prepare, cook and sieve as for lentil purée, but add 20 mins to cooking time to ensure that they are completely soft.

Sprout

5 small brussels sprouts

Trim off any blemished outer leaves and wash sprouts in salted water. Bring about 1 inch (3 cm) water to the boil, add sprouts, cover and simmer until tender, 7–12 mins. Drain, chop roughly and put through a hand blender.

Swede

1 small or ½ medium swede

Scrub and peel swede. Dice and put into about 1 inch (3 cm) boiling water and simmer, covered, until tender, about 20 mins. Drain, saving liquid. Mash finely with a fork, adding a little cooking liquid if too thick.

Sweet Pepper

1 red or green sweet pepper

Wash pepper, cut in half and remove stalks, seeds and pith. Cube and put into 1 inch (3 cm) boiling water. Simmer with lid on for 5 mins. Drain, put through a hand blender. (Peppers have a high Vitamin C content.)

Tomato

1 tomato

Plunge tomato into boiling water for 30 seconds, then peel. Press through sieve and discard seeds or remove seeds and put through a hand blender.
or
1 Italian tinned tomato

Press drained tomato through a sieve, discarding seeds and any skin or fibres. It can be thinned with juice from the tin.

Turnip

1 small turnip

Wash, scrub, peel and dice turnip. Bring 1 inch (3 cm) water to the boil. Simmer, covered, until tender, 15–20 mins. Mash with a fork until smooth.

Fruit Purées

Apple

1 small cooking apple   ½ tbsp sugar

Wash, peel, core and quarter apple. Bring to boil just covered with water and a lid. Simmer until soft. Add the sugar – just enough to prevent tartness, and stir gently until dissolved. Drain off juice (for drinking when cool). Mash apple with a fork.

or

1 eating apple

Wash, peel finely, core and roughly chop apple. Whizz with 2–3 tbsps water in an electric liquidizer until smooth.

Apricot

6 dried or fresh apricots

Wash dried apricots and soak overnight. Bring to the boil and simmer until the skins are tender, 30–45 mins. If a trace of sugar is necessary to prevent tartness, add just before removing from the heat and stir gently to dissolve. (If added too soon, the fruit will not soften.)

Wash and dry fresh apricots carefully. Cut in half, remove stones, bring to the boil just covered with water and simmer until tender, 15–30 mins.

Drain off the juice for a drink, and press apricots through a sieve, discarding the skins.

Banana

½ ripe banana

Peel and mash smooth with a fork.

Blackcurrant

2 tbsps (about 1 oz, 25 g) fresh   3 tbsps water
  or frozen blackcurrants   ½ teasp sugar

Wash blackcurrants if fresh. Simmer fruit with sugar and water
for 15 mins. Press through a sieve, discarding the skins. This
makes a very rich, slightly tart purée which is probably better
diluted with a little baby milk at first. It is, of course, very rich in
Vitamin C.

Fig

4 figs, dried

Wash, soak overnight, bring to the boil and simmer until tender,
about 20 mins. Drain. Press through a sieve, discarding the
seeds, stalks and any coarse skin.

Grape

6–8 green or black grapes

Wash well, peel, halve and remove seeds. Mash with a fork
until smooth or press through a sieve.

Grapefruit

½ small or ¼ large grapefruit

Peel, remove pips, pith and divide into segments. Whizz in an
electric liquidizer adding 1 or 2 tbsps water if necessary. If your
baby is averse to tartness, add ½ teasp honey and blend again to
mix.

Melon

1 wedge ripe melon, about 3 oz (75 g)

Remove seeds, peel and dice melon. Mash smooth with a fork
or put through a hand blender.

Orange

½ orange

Remove peel, pith and pips. Divide into segments. Whizz in an
electric liquidizer, adding 1 or 2 tbsps water if necessary, until
pulped.

Peach

1 ripe peach

Wash and dry peach. Peel, halve, remove stone and mash with a
fork.

Pear

1 soft ripe pear

Wash, peel, quarter and remove core. Mash smooth with a fork.

Plum

5 sweet soft plums

Wash, peel, halve and remove stones. Mash smooth with a fork.

or

5 cooking plums   ½ teasp or so sugar, or honey

Wash, halve, remove stones and bring to the boil in just enough
water to cover. Simmer until tender, 15–20 mins. Before re-

moving from heat, add just enough sugar or honey to prevent tartness, if necessary, and stir until it dissolves. Drain, saving the juice, and put plums through a sieve, discarding skins.

Prune

6 prunes

Soak overnight. Bring to the boil just covered with water and simmer until soft, 20–30 mins. Drain, saving juice for a drink, remove stones and press through sieve or mash with a fork.

Raisin or Sultana

10–15 seedless raisins or sultanas

Soak fruit overnight. Bring to the boil just covered with water and simmer until plump and tender, 15–20 mins. Drain, press through a sieve or put through a hand blender.

Meat Purées

Quick Beef

2–3 oz (75 g) lean roasting or   1 tbsp baby milk or water
grilling beef

Shred raw beef finely by scraping it with a finely serrated steak knife, or pulp it with an electric chopper. Put pulped meat with 1 tbsp baby milk or water between two plates, or a plate and lid, over a pan of simmering water, until the meat changes colour, about 5 mins. Put, with milk or water, through a hand blender, adding a little more liquid if necessary to make a smooth purée.

Stewed Beef

2–3 oz (75 g) lean stewing beef

Make sure all fat is trimmed off meat then cut into small pieces or mince in a mincer or electric chopper. Bring to the boil slowly, just covered with water and simmer, covered, until tender, 15–45 mins, depending on size.

Drain meat, saving liquid, and put through a hand blender, adding enough cooking liquid to make a smooth purée.

Chicken

½ breast of chicken   1 tbsp baby milk or water

Wash, dry and remove skin of chicken. Shred by scraping with a serrated knife, or slice finely. Put shredded chicken with 1 tbsp water or baby milk between two plates, or a plate and lid, over a pan of simmering water until the chicken is tender and cooked, 5–15 mins.

Put through a hand blender with the cooking milk or water, adding a little more liquid if too thick.

Heart

1 chicken heart or 2–3 oz (75 g) beef or lamb's heart

Wash heart and squeeze out all blood. Cut up, cook and blend as for Stewed Beef purée.

Kidney

1 small lamb's kidney or ½ veal kidney

Remove fat, skin and hard core from kidney. Wash and dry. Slice and bring to the boil, just covered with cold water. Simmer, covered, until tender, about 15 mins. Drain, saving liquid.

Put through a hand blender and add enough of the cooking liquid to make a smooth purée.

Quick Lamb

2–3 oz (75 g) lean roasting or   1 tbsp baby milk or water
  grilling lamb

Shred, pulp, cook and purée lamb as for Quick Beef Purée.

Stewed Lamb

2–3 oz (75 g) lean stewing lamb

Cut up, cook and purée as for Stewed Beef Purée.

Liver

2–3 oz (75 g) lamb's, calf's,   1 tbsp baby milk or water
  pig's or chicken's liver

Wash carefully and dry liver, then cut away any coarse connective tissue. Pulp liver by scraping a knife over its surface, pressing slightly to break it up. Cook with milk or water between two plates, or a plate and lid, over a pan of simmering water, until it changes colour, about 5 mins. Put through a hand blender with milk or water, adding more liquid if too thick.

Sweetbreads or Brains

1 pair sweetbreads or 1 set   1–2 tbsps baby milk
  lamb's or calf's brains

Soak sweetbreads or brains in cold water for about 1 hr until all the blood is removed. Remove skin and coarse fibres.

  Cover sweetbreads or brains with fresh cold water and bring slowly to the boil. Simmer, covered, for 2 mins, then throw water away. Re-cover with cold water, bring slowly to the boil, with lid on, and simmer again until tender, about 15 mins. Drain.

Put through a hand blender and combine with baby milk until it is the right consistency.

Tongue

1 sheep's tongue

Wash and soak the tongue in cold water for 2 hrs. Bring to the boil covered with fresh cold water, simmer for 2 mins, then pour water away. Bring to the boil again covered with water, and simmer until tender, 1–1½ hrs. Drain and save liquid. Remove skin from tongue, chop roughly and put through a hand blender, or whizz with 2 or 3 tbsps of the cooking liquid in an electric blender until smooth.

Fish, Egg and Cheese Purées

Fish

1–3 oz (75 g) filleted white fish   2 tbsps baby milk or water

Wash and dry fish (fresh or frozen, such as cod, haddock, coley, sole or plaice). Put fish and milk or water between two plates, or a plate and lid, over a pan of simmering water until fish separates easily into flakes, 20–30 mins.

Remove any skin from fish and check for stray bones. Put through a hand blender with the milk or water and mix with a little more liquid if too thick.

Egg Yolk

1 egg

Separate white from yolk by breaking shell in half and passing yolk from one half to the other, allowing the white to drain into a cup.

Put the yolk into a heatproof basin or cup, set this in a pan of water that has just boiled and stir until it is heated and just beginning to thicken, a few seconds. (Save the white for an adult dish. It is better to give yolk only to babies under 8 mths.)

or

Hard-boil the egg by bringing to the boil in a small saucepan, covered with cold water, and a drop of vinegar to help prevent the shell from cracking. Simmer for 10 mins. Cool in cold water, shell, halve and remove yolk. Mash yolk with a fork, press through sieve or put through a hand blender. Add 1 tbsp baby milk or more to make a smooth purée.

Cottage Cheese

1 tbsp cottage cheese   ½ tbsp baby milk

Put cottage cheese through a hand blender or sieve and mix with enough baby milk to make a smooth purée.

Cheddar Cheese

½ oz (12 g) mild Cheddar cheese   1 tbsp water that has just boiled

Put cheese through a hand blender, add freshly boiled water and stir until cheese is dissolved. (This is a very easy way of making a cheese sauce for babies of all ages – just double, treble or whatever, the quantities.)

Using up Left-overs

Vegetable and Meat Purées

Add to family soups, stews and casseroles. Or combine with egg, breadcrumbs and herbs to make rissoles.

Meat purées beaten with butter, seasoning and herbs or spices make very good spreads or quick pâtés.

Fruit Purées

Delicious poured on ice cream or sponge pudding, whisked with milk for a fruity shake, or set into a jelly.

Egg and Cheese Purées

Stir into savoury sauces and soups just before serving, or combine with butter, seasoning and herbs for a sandwich spread.

Nutritious Meat Dishes

These recipes are specially devised to meet the needs of those who want to provide a main course for one baby at midday, perhaps because the family eats in the evening. The quantities, therefore, are the smallest practical for one, but until your baby's appetite develops, there will probably be enough for part of your lunch too.

The preponderance of ways with liver is deliberate, as it is especially nutritious – so if one is rejected, do try another. But that goes for all the recipes!

Taffy's Stew

2–3 oz (75 g) lean beef
1 small carrot
1 small potato

1 tomato
1 small stick celery
dash salt for babies over 8 mths

Cut beef into small pieces. Clean, peel and dice carrot and potato. Skin, de-seed and chop tomato. Clean and chop celery.

Put all ingredients into a small pan, with salt if used, bring to the boil, just covered with water, and simmer with the lid on until cooked, 20–30 mins.

For babies under 6 mths, drain, keeping liquid hot, put through a hand blender and mix with enough of the cooking liquid to make a smooth purée.

For older babies, mash or not according to stage reached, and serve with any green vegetable from 'Purées Galore'.

Shepherd's Pie

2–3 oz (75 g) lean stewing beef
  or lamb
1 small potato
1–2 tbsps baby milk or water

1 teasp or so baby cereal for
  babies over 6 mths
dot butter
dash salt for babies over 8 mths

Mince meat in a mincer or electric chopper (or prepare butcher's
minced meat as in Minced Beef Casserole, page 120), and simmer,
with salt, if used, just covered with water, until tender, 25–30
mins.

Peel and grate potato and cook with milk or water on a lightly
buttered plate over the simmering meat, covered with the pan
lid, until tender 20–25 mins.

For babies under 6 mths, drain meat, keep the liquid warm,
and put meat through a hand blender. Mash potatoes well and
mix with blended meat and enough of the cooking liquid or baby
milk to give a smooth consistency.

For older babies, thicken meaty cooking liquid with a little
baby cereal and spread mashed potato over the meat. (Fork over,
put in a small casserole and grill until attractively golden on top,
if this is likely to be appreciated.)

Serve with carrot and a green vegetable.

Irish Stew

2–3 oz (75 g) lean stewing
  lamb
1 potato

1 slice onion for babies over
  8 mths
dash salt for babies over 8 mths

Cut meat into small pieces. Peel and thinly slice potato and chop
onion very small. Put meat, onion and potato into a small pan
in layers, finishing with potato. Add salt, if used, and enough
water to come half-way up the meat and potato. Bring to the boil
and simmer gently until both meat and potatoes are tender,
1–2 hrs.

For babies under 6 mths, drain, keep liquid hot, and put meat and potato through a hand blender, adding enough cooking liquid to give the right consistency.

For older babies, mash or chop according to stage reached, and serve with peas or green beans.

Grilled Cutlet

1 small lamb chop   dot butter
½ teasp baby cereal

Trim fat from chop. Wash and dry it. Smear lightly with butter, place on a rack in a clean grill pan and cook 3 inches (8 cm) from medium grill until chop is cooked half-way through, 4–5 mins. Turn, smear the other side with butter and grill until brown and cooked right through. Remove from heat, pour juices from grill pan into a cup to cool, skim off fat and reheat.

For babies under 7 mths, cut meat from bone, put through a hand blender and mix with cooking juices.

For older babies, cut meat from bone and dice. Thicken meat juices with the baby cereal and pour over meat. Serve with spinach or peas.

Mince Bake

2–3 oz (75 g) lean beef or lamb   2 tbsps water
1 small turnip   dash salt for babies over 8 mths
1 carrot   dot butter
1 slice onion for babies over
   8 mths

Put meat through a fine mincer, mince in an electric chopper or cut very small. Peel and dice turnip and carrot. Chop small or grate onion, if used. Mix all ingredients and put into a small, lightly buttered casserole. Add water and bake, covered with lid or foil, at 350°F (180°C) Gas 4, or steam, until cooked, about 1 hr.

For babies under 6 mths put through a hand blender.

Creamed Chicken

1 breast chicken   ½ teasp or so baby rice
1 stalk celery

Skin, wash, dry and dice chicken. Clean and dice celery and put on top of chicken in a small pan with water just covering chicken. Simmer, with lid on, until tender, 20–30 mins. Drain, keeping the liquid warm.

For babies under 6 mths, put chicken and celery through a hand blender and add a little baby rice mixed with 1–2 tbsps of the cooking liquid.

For older babies, mash or cut the chicken and celery to an acceptable size. Thicken some of the cooking liquid with a little baby rice and add chicken and celery.

Serve with sprouts or cabbage.

Chicken and Apricots

5 dried apricots   dot butter
1 tbsp water   dash salt for babies over 8 mths
2–3 oz (75 g) bone-free chicken   1 dessertsp or so baby rice
  (breast, wing or leg)   (optional)

Wash apricots and soak overnight. Bring to the boil slowly and simmer gently until tender, 15–30 mins. Meantime, wash and dry the chicken, remove skin, smear with butter and cook on a plate with the water, covered by another plate, with salt, if used, over the simmering apricots until tender, 30–45 mins.

For babies under 6 mths, put chicken and drained apricots through a hand blender.

For older babies, serve chicken and apricots drained (save the juice for a drink), cut to an acceptable size. If your baby likes sauces, thicken a few tbsps of the juice with baby cereal, heat gently, and serve with chicken and apricot.

Grilled Chicken and Peas

1 breast chicken	3 tbsps fresh or frozen peas
few drops vegetable oil	

Wash, dry and skin chicken breast. Smear lightly with oil and grill under a medium heat on a rack in a clean grill pan. When half done, 4–5 mins, turn, lightly oil the other side and finish cooking.

Meantime, put peas into about 1 inch (3 cm) boiling water and simmer until cooked, 5–12 mins.

For babies under 6 mths, cut up grilled chicken and put through a hand blender with the peas.

For older babies, cut chicken to an acceptable size and mash peas or not as necessary.

Chicken in Foil with Tomatoes

1 chicken breast, leg or wing	1 teasp or so baby cereal for
dot butter	babies over 6 mths
2 tomatoes	dash salt for babies over 8 mths

Wash and dry chicken piece, smear with butter and place in a heatproof dish on a piece of aluminium foil big enough to wrap round it. Make a thickish purée with the tomatoes, as in 'Purées Galore', and spoon this over the chicken, adding salt if used. Wrap the foil round closely and bake at 360°F (185°C), Gas 4–5, until tender, about 30 mins. Remove skin and cut chicken away from the bone if necessary.

For babies under 6 mths, put chicken through a hand blender and mix with enough of the liquid in the foil to make a smooth purée.

For older babies, cut meat to an acceptable size. Mix liquid from the foil with a little baby cereal to make a sauce and reheat this gently with the chicken. Sprouts, peas or beans go well with this.

Ham and Beans

(for babies over 8 mths)

2–3 oz (75 g) very lean ham   4 or 5 pods fresh or equivalent
1 potato   in frozen green beans

If salty, soak ham in cold water for 3–5 hrs. Dice, just cover with cold water and bring to the boil. Add the potato, peeled and diced. Simmer together for 5 mins. Add prepared beans and continue cooking until all ingredients are tender, 7–10 mins. Drain, and serve ham, potato and beans as they are or mashed, according to your baby's taste.

Veal Blanquette

2–3 oz (75 g) stewing veal   1 stalk celery
dash salt for babies over 8 mths   ½–1 teasp baby rice
1 slice finely chopped onion for   1–2 drops lemon juice
   babies over 8 mths   1 teasp egg yolk
1 small carrot

Wash and dry veal and cut in small pieces. Put in a pan with salt and onion, if used, then add cleaned, sliced carrot and celery and enough water to cover veal. Simmer, covered, until tender, about 1 hr.

Drain off liquid and mix enough of this with the baby rice to make a thickish sauce. Reheat, adding lemon juice and egg yolk, but do not allow to boil.

For babies under 6 mths, put veal and vegetables through a blender before mixing with some of the sauce.

For older babies chop veal to an acceptable size, mash vegetables or not according to stage reached before adding to sauce.

Serve with tomatoes, peeled and de-seeded, and/or cabbage.

Braised Brains and Broccoli

1 set lamb's or calf's brains
dash salt for babies over 8 mths
1 small potato
1 tbsp baby milk or water

2–3 sprigs fresh or frozen
 broccoli
1–2 drops lemon juice

Prepare and cook brains as in 'Purées Galore' with salt, if used. Peel and grate potato finely and cook with the milk or water on a lightly buttered plate over the brains, covered. Wash broccoli, put into 1 inch (3 cm) boiling water and simmer until tender, 10–15 mins.

For babies under 6 mths put brains and broccoli through a hand blender, mash the potato well and mix with the blended brains and broccoli.

For older babies, cut the brains to an acceptable size and serve with mashed potato and broccoli, mashed or chopped.

Hearty Tomato

2–3 oz (75 g) beef heart
1 large or 2 small tomatoes

½–1 teasp baby cereal
dash salt for babies over 8 mths

Prepare, cook and purée heart and tomatoes as in 'Purées Galore'. Mix together, adding enough tomato juice and baby cereal to give the right consistency for babies under 6 mths. Reheat gently with salt if used.

For older babies, chop heart to an acceptable size and stir into a sauce made with the tomato purée and baby cereal. Add salt and reheat gently.

Kidney Special

1 lamb's kidney
1 potato
1 carrot

1 tomato
dash salt for babies over 8 mths

Remove fat, skin and hard core from the kidney and wash and

dry it. Slice, and put in a pan with the potato and carrot, peeled and diced, and the tomato peeled (plunge into boiling water for 30 secs to loosen skin), de-seeded and chopped. Cover with cold water, adding salt, if used, and simmer until tender, 15–20 mins. Drain.

For babies under 6 mths put through a hand blender and mix with enough of the cooking liquid to give the right consistency.

For older babies mash or chop according to stage reached and serve with a green vegetable if your baby's appetite demands it.

Kidney and Beef Pâté
(for babies over 8 mths)

1 small lamb's kidney	1 teasp egg yolk
2 oz (50 g) lean beef	1 slice onion
1 heaped tbsp brown breadcrumbs	dash salt
1 tomato	few drops vegetable oil

Remove fat, skin and hard core from kidney and wash and dry it. Mince beef and kidney in a mincer or electric chopper or cut in small pieces. Combine beef and kidney with breadcrumbs, tomato, puréed as in 'Purées Galore', egg yolk, finely chopped onion and salt.

Bake at 350°F (180°C), Gas 4, or steam, in a small, lightly oiled casserole covered with lid or foil, for 1 hr, or until meat is tender.

Serve sliced or diced with a green vegetable.

Liver Mash

2–3 oz (75 g) lamb's, calf's or ox liver
1 potato

dash salt for babies over 8 mths
2–3 tbsps baby milk or water
few drops vegetable oil

Wash and dry liver and pulp it by scraping and pressing it with a knife, discarding any coarse connective tissue;
or
Cut away the connective tissue and put the liver through a hand blender. Wash and scrub the potato and boil, covered, unpeeled, until tender, 20–30 mins. Put the pulped liver with salt, if used, on a lightly oiled plate over the potato pan, covered with the lid, for the last 5 mins of the cooking time, until the liver changes colour.

Put liver through a hand blender, peel and mash the potato and combine the two with enough heated milk or water to give the right consistency.

Serve with a green vegetable.

Liver Cheese

2–3 oz (75 g) lamb's, calf's or ox liver
1 small potato

1 dessertsp cottage cheese or grated mild Cheddar cheese

Prepare, cook and purée liver and potato as above.

For babies under 6 mths purée the cheese as in 'Purées Galore' and stir into liver and potato.

For older babies, just stir cheese into liver mixture. (The cheese gives the liver an interesting lift in flavour.)

Liver and Tomato

2–3 oz (75 g) liver	½–1 teasp baby rice
2 tomatoes	dash salt for babies over 8 mths

Wash and dry the liver and cut away any coarse connective tissue, then cut in smallish pieces. Purée the tomatoes as in 'Purées Galore', page 35, and put in a pan with the liver, salt, if used, and 2 tbsps water. Bring to the boil, slowly, and simmer until the liver is tender, about 10 mins. Drain and keep liquid warm.

For babies under 6 mths put through a hand blender and mix with enough of the cooking juices and baby rice to give a smooth consistency.

For older babies, mash or chop according to stage reached and mix cooking liquid with enough baby rice to make a sauce in which to serve the liver.

Liver and Beef Pâté

(for babies over 8 mths)

2 oz (50 g) liver	1 teasp egg yolk
2 oz (50 g) lean beef	dash salt
1 carrot	1 tbsp brown breadcrumbs
1 slice onion	few drops vegetable oil

Wash and dry liver, cut away any skin, tubes or connective tissue and put through a hand blender. Mince beef in mincer or electric chopper, or cut in very small pieces. Wash, peel and grate carrot and onion.

Combine liver, beef, carrot, onion, egg yolk, salt and breadcrumbs. Spoon into a small, lightly oiled casserole, cover with lid or foil, and bake at 350°F (180°C), Gas 4, or steam, for 1 hr. Serve sliced or diced with spinach or peas. (Liver, even if rejected in other forms, is often accepted this way.)

Liver Casserole

2–3 oz (75 g) lamb's, calf's or
  ox liver
1 small carrot
½ small turnip

1 slice swede
2 slices onion for babies over
  8 mths
dash salt for babies over 8 mths

Wash, dry, cut connective tissue away from liver and dice it.
Peel and dice carrot, turnip and swede. Chop onion small, if
used. Put all vegetables in pan with 1 inch (3 cm) boiling water
and simmer, covered, with salt if used, adding diced liver for
last 10 mins of cooking time. Drain, and keep liquid warm.

For babies under 6 mths put through a blender and add
enough cooking liquid to give a smooth consistency. For older
babies, mash or chop according to stage reached, thickening
some of the cooking liquid with baby cereal if there is no weight
problem.

Creamed Sweetbread

1 small sheep's sweetbread
dash salt for babies over 8 mths

1–3 teasps baby rice
1–2 tbsps baby milk

Soak the sweetbread in cold water for 1 hr to remove blood. Then
strain and simmer covered with water for 1 min. Drain and cool
sweetbread in cold water before removing skin and fibres. Bring
to the boil again, just covered with water, with salt if used, and
simmer for 1 hr. Drain, and save cooking liquid.

For babies under 6 mths, put the sweetbread through a hand
blender and mix with a little cooking liquid and baby rice to give
a smooth consistency.

For older babies, chop sweetbread to an acceptable size. Mix
baby rice with a few tbsps cooking liquid or baby milk and bring
to the boil. Add the sweetbreads and serve, accompanied by
carrot and/or peas, or tomatoes, peeled, de-seeded and chopped.

55

Tongue and Tomato

1 sheep's tongue   2 tomatoes

Prepare, cook and skin tongue as in 'Purées Galore', but only purée for babies under 6 or 7 mths, otherwise chop tongue to acceptable size. Purée tomatoes as in 'Purées Galore' and combine with puréed or chopped tongue over a gentle heat.

    Serve with peas or beans.

Ideas for Fish

Fish is also very nutritious and from about four months most babies will take to it happily, simply puréed as in 'Purées Galore'.

Here are some recipes for the next stage. Although the quantities are as small as can reasonably be cooked there will be more than a very young baby can consume, so the recipes should provide a fish snack for you too, at any rate at first.

Poached Fillet with Peas

1 small fillet (2–3 oz, 75 g) cod, haddock, coley, sole, plaice or other white fish, fresh or frozen	dash salt for babies over 8 mths 2 tbsps water or baby milk 4 tbsps fresh or frozen peas dot butter

Wash and dry fish and put with milk or water and salt, if used, between 2 plates, or on a plate covered with the lid, over a pan of simmering water until the flakes separate easily, 20–30 mins. Add peas to simmering water after 10 mins of cooking time, turning up the heat if necessary to bring back to a simmer, and cook until tender, 5–12 mins. Drain fish, check for stray bones, skin if necessary.

For babies under 6 mths, put both fish and peas through a hand blender, adding a little of the cooking liquid to give a smooth consistency.

For older babies, mash or flake fish according to stage reached, and serve, moistened with some of the milky cooking liquid and peas, mashed or whole.

Fish Pie

1 frozen brick cod or haddock	1 teasp grated mild Cheddar cheese
1 potato	dash salt for babies over 8 mths

Steam fish, with salt if used, until flakes separate easily with a fork, about 20 mins. At the same time cook potato, peeled and cubed, below steamer, until tender. Skin fish if necessary and check for stray bones.

For a baby under 6 mths, put as much fish and grated cheese as she is likely to eat through a hand blender and mix with the mashed potato and enough of the cooking liquid to give a smooth consistency.

For older babies, mash fish and potato with grated cheese, adding a little cooking liquid or milk as necessary. (If it is likely to be appreciated, spoon the mixture into a small, lightly greased, heatproof dish, fork over the top and pop under a medium grill until it is attractively golden.)

Serve with spinach or another green vegetable.

Fish and Tomato Purée in Foil

1 frozen brick cod or haddock	dash salt for babies over 8 mths
2 tomatoes or 1 tbsp tomato purée	1–4 teasps baby cereal

If using tomatoes, make a thickish purée as in 'Purées Galore'. Place the fish, still frozen, on a piece of foil large enough to wrap round it, in a baking tin. Spoon over the tomato purée, add salt if used, and wrap up well. Bake at 350°F (180°C), Gas 4, or steam, until the flakes separate easily when tested with a fork, about 25–30 mins. Drain fish and save liquid. Check for stray bones.

For babies under 6 mths, put only as much fish as your baby is likely to eat through a hand blender and mix with enough of the tomato cooking juices and baby cereal to give a smooth consistency.

For older babies, pour the cooking liquid from the foil into a pan and mix with enough baby cereal to make a thickish sauce. Mash or flake the fish according to stage reached and combine with the sauce, warming all together gently before serving if necessary.

Carrots go well with this.

Cod in Cheese Sauce

1 small fillet or frozen cod brick (about 2–3 oz, 75 g)

1 oz (25 g) mild Cheddar cheese
2 tbsps baby milk or water

Wash and dry fish, then simmer slowly, just covered with water, until it flakes easily when a fork is inserted. Drain, check for stray bones, skin if necessary and mash or flake.

While fish is cooking, put the cheese through a hand blender, bring the milk or water to the boil, pour over the cheese and stir. Add flaked or mashed fish.

Serve with swede and a green vegetable. For babies under 6 mths, put through a hand blender.

Haddock with Orange

1 small haddock fillet or a frozen haddock brick (about 2–3 oz, 75 g)
juice of a small orange
½ tbsp grated mild Cheddar cheese

1 teasp crushed cornflake crumbs
dot butter
1–2 teasps baby rice (optional)

Wash and dry haddock and place in a lightly greased heatproof dish. Pour the orange juice over, sprinkle with cheese and corn-flake crumbs, dot with butter and cover with foil. Bake at 350°F (180°C), Gas 4, or steam, until flakes separate easily, 25–30 mins. Drain fish and save liquid. Check carefully for stray bones.

For babies under 6 mths, put as much of the fish and cheese as he is likely to eat through a hand blender and mix with enough of the orange liquid to give a smooth consistency.

For older babies, mash or flake the fish, thicken the sauce with baby rice, reheat gently. Add the fish and serve with a green or root vegetable.

Creamed Fish and Cauliflower

1 small fillet fish such as cod, haddock, plaice or sole (about 2–3 oz, 75 g) fresh or frozen	2 sprigs cauliflower 1–2 dessertsps baby rice dash salt for babies over 8 mths

Prepare and cook fish as in Poached Fillet with Peas, adding washed cauliflower instead of peas to the simmering water after 10 mins of cooking time. Cook until tender, 7–10 mins. Drain fish, saving liquid, and check carefully for stray bones. Drain cauliflower.

For babies under 6 mths, put fish and cauliflower through a hand blender and stir in enough of the cooking liquid and baby rice to give a smooth consistency.

For older babies, mash or flake fish and mash or chop cauli-flower roughly. Mix cooking liquid from fish with the baby rice, adding more milk or water if necessary for a runnier sauce. Stir fish and cauliflower into sauce over a low heat, adding a dash of salt.

Nursery Kedgeree

½ tbsp freshly cooked
  bone-free fish or 1 tbsp flaked
  tuna or salmon from a tin
1 dessertsp raw rice or 2 tbsps
  freshly cooked rice

½ hard-boiled egg yolk
dot butter
1 tbsp baby milk
dash salt for babies over 8 mths

If raw, wash rice well in a sieve under cold running water, then put into 3 ins (8 cm) fast boiling water in a small pan and simmer for 13 mins. Drain, wash in a sieve under cold water again. Combine cooked rice and fish. Melt butter in a small pan, stir in fish, rice, baby milk and salt, if used, over a low heat until it is thoroughly heated.

For babies under 6 mths put through a hand blender.

Serve topped with sieved egg yolk or stir this into the kedgeree if it is more likely to be acceptable this way.

Fish Patty

(for babies over 8 mths)

2 tbsps flaked and drained
  salmon or tuna from a tin
1 tbsp boiling water
2 tbsps brown breadcrumbs

1 dessertsp grated cheese
dash salt
dot butter

Pour boiled water over breadcrumbs and stir in flaked fish, cheese and salt. Turn mixture into a lightly buttered small, shallow heatproof dish, dot with butter and pop under a medium grill until heated right through, 10–15 mins.

Fish Mould

2 tbsps white fish, freshly
   cooked, bone-free and flaked
1 level tbsp cornflakes
1 small slice onion for babies
   over 8 mths

1 teasp egg yolk
2 tbsps baby milk
dash salt for babies over 8 mths

Crush cornflakes, chop onion finely and put cooked fish through a hand blender. Beat egg, add milk, fish, salt, if used, and cornflakes. Spoon into a lightly greased casserole, cover with foil and bake at 350°F (180°C), Gas 4, or steam until set, 25–30 mins.

Serve with tomatoes, peeled, de-seeded and chopped, carrots or a green vegetable.

Mini Fish Cakes

1 frozen brick cod or haddock,
   or 2–3 oz (75 g) filleted white
   fish
1 potato
1 teasp egg yolk
¼ teasp finely ground parsley

1–2 drops lemon juice
dot butter
1 dessertsp fine breadcrumbs or
   crushed cornflakes
dash salt for babies over 8 mths

Prepare fish and potato as for Fish Pie, page 58. Drain potatoes and mash both with the egg yolk, parsley and lemon juice. Form into small cakes, smear lightly with butter and sprinkle with crumbs. Grill under a medium heat, turning once, for 15–20 mins.

For babies under 6 mths mash or put through a hand blender.

Dice for babies feeding themselves and serve with green beans.

Roes in Egg Sauce

2 oz (50 g) soft herring roes	1 tbsp baby cereal
1 cup (approx) baby milk	1 teasp egg yolk

Wash roes under running cold water then simmer slowly, covered with milk, until tender, about 10 mins. Drain, saving liquid, allow to cool a little and remove skins.

For babies under 6 mths, put roes through a hand blender.

For older babies mix the baby cereal with some cooking liquid to make a sauce, stir in the egg yolk, add the roes blended or chopped, and heat together without allowing to boil.

Serve with rusks or toast fingers and mashed potato.

Simple Soups

Soups can be an excellent way of drinking nourishment – serve them in a cup when your baby is ready.

All these are very easy to make, but for the liquid, use only the salt-free stocks referred to below, Baby Soup Stock from 'Meals to Freeze', or water. Any milk in the recipe should be baby dried milk, mixed exactly according to instructions on the pack, or for babies over five months half ordinary liquid cow's milk and half water. Undiluted liquid cow's milk can be used for babies over eight months.

Small Stocks

Most soups include stock, but as adult stock and cubes are too highly seasoned and flavoured for babies, you cannot use these.

So, unless you have a freezer (see Baby Soup Stock in 'Foods to Freeze') or you are making stock for the family anyway, and take out a portion for your baby before adding seasoning, herbs, spices, onion and other strong flavouring, it is not worth making special stock for these recipes. There are several easy ways of obtaining a small quantity of nutritious stock for a baby, however, most of which are meat soups in themselves.

1. *From grilled or roast meat*
Make sure grill or roast pan is clean before cooking meat and do not add seasoning or strong flavourings to the meat (not until later anyway).

When meat is almost cooked, put it on one side to keep warm while you add 1–2 cups water to pan (depending on size), mix well with the meat juices and pour enough for baby into a cup to cool.

Meantime return the meat to finish cooking, adding seasoning and any other flavourings for the family.

Skim fat off the cooled liquid, strain if necessary, and bring it to the boil. Use on its own or in a soup.

2. *From the family roast*

Do not add salt or strong flavourings at first. About two thirds of the way through cooking time, remove meat from the oven and press a dessertspoon into meat, allowing meat juices to run into it. Pour into a cup and allow to cool. Skim off fat and strain if necessary.

Place this stock in a small pan with as much water as there is meat juice and bring to the boil, or add to a soup and boil before serving.

3. *From braised or stewed meat*

Omit seasoning and other strong flavouring for the family at first. About three quarters of the way through cooking time, remove a few tbsps liquid for your baby and allow to cool. Meantime, add seasoning and other flavouring to the braise or stew for the family and continue cooking.

Skim fat off the cooled liquid, strain if necessary, bring to the boil, then serve as it is or use as stock.

4. *From cooking vegetables*

Use any liquid in which vegetables such as those in 'Purées Galore' have just been cooked, provided no seasoning or strong flavourings have been added before removing what is needed for your baby.

65

Vegetable Broth

¼ pint (5 fl oz, 125 ml) stock or
water
½ cup mixed diced vegetables
(carrot, swede, celery, turnip)

1 small leaf cabbage
dash salt for babies over 8 mths

Simmer all vegetables except cabbage, covered with stock or
water, and salt if used, for 10–15 mins until almost cooked. Add
cabbage, washed and finely shredded and continue to cook for a
further 7 mins or until all the vegetables are tender.

Whizz in a liquidizer or sieve or blend to make a smooth
puréed broth.

Cream of Pea Soup

2 oz (5 tbsps, 50 g) freshly
shelled or frozen peas
3 fl oz (5 tbsps, 75 ml) water or
stock

2–3 fl oz (5 tbsps, 75 ml) baby
milk

Bring water or stock to the boil, add peas and simmer until
tender, 5–8 mins. Either whizz in an electric liquidizer with milk
until smooth, or drain peas, saving liquid, and put them through
a sieve or hand blender, before stirring into the cooking liquid
and milk. Reheat soup until just boiling before serving.

Cream of Tomato Soup

2 large or 3 small tomatoes
2–4 tbsps baby milk
dash salt for babies over 8 mths

2–4 tbsps stock (optional)
1 tbsp yogurt (optional)

Make a thin purée of the tomatoes as in 'Purées Galore', stir
with the milk. Heat, adding salt and stock, if used, just bringing
to the boil. Stir in yogurt, if used, just before serving.

Lentil Soup

2 tbsps red lentils
1 slice onion (for babies over 8 mths)
1 small carrot

$\frac{2}{5}$ pint (8 fl oz, 200 ml) water or stock
2–4 tbsps baby milk (optional)

Wash lentils. Chop onion finely, peel and dice carrot. Simmer lentils and vegetables in the water or stock until lentils are very soft, 30–45 mins, adding more liquid if necessary. Reheat, adding milk if used, until just boiling.

Chicken and Celery Soup

2 oz approx (50 g) bone-free chicken (breast, wing or leg)
1 stalk celery

1 small slice onion for babies over 8 mths
dash salt for babies over 8 mths

Remove skin, wash, dry and dice chicken small. Clean and chop celery and chop onion finely. Simmer together, covered with water and a lid, until all the ingredients are cooked and tender, 20–30 mins.

For babies under 6 mths either whizz in an electric liquidizer until smooth, or put drained chicken and vegetables through a hand blender and return to cooking liquid. Either way, reheat before serving.

For older babies who are taking lumpy food, serve as it is, with salt.

Cream of Carrot Soup

1 carrot
3 fl oz (5 tbsps, 75 ml) stock or water

dash salt for babies over 8 mths
$\frac{1}{4}$ pint (5 fl oz, 125 ml) baby milk

Clean, peel and slice carrot, and simmer in stock or water until tender, with salt if used, about 10–15 mins. Drain and keep cooking liquid.

Mash carrot finely, add milk and reheat with enough of the cooking liquid to give the right consistency for your baby.

Cream of Spinach Soup

4–5 leaves spinach or 2–3 oz
   (75 g) frozen spinach
3 tbsps stock (optional)

1 cup baby milk
dash salt for babies over 8 mths

Prepare, cook (with stock if used) and purée spinach as in 'Purées Galore'. Add milk and heat with salt, if used, just bringing to the boil.

Baby Bortsch

1 small beetroot
¼ pint (5 fl oz, 125 ml) baby
   milk

drop lemon juice

Prepare, cook and purée beetroot as in 'Purées Galore'. Combine with milk and bring slowly to the boil. Stir in a drop of lemon juice after removing from the heat.

Serve warm or cold, chilling quickly by standing in cold or iced water to cool, then in a refrigerator.

Mini Minestrone

½ cup mixed diced vegetables
   (carrot, swede, celery, etc.)
½ pint (10 fl oz, 250 ml) stock
   or water
dash salt for babies over 8 mths
2 tomatoes

1 leaf fresh (or equivalent in
   frozen) spinach
½ oz (12 g) macaroni or other
   small pasta
1 dessertsp finely grated cheese

Simmer vegetables in stock or water for 15 mins with salt, if used. Make a thin purée of tomatoes, as in 'Purées Galore', wash and shred spinach finely and wash pasta. Add these to the soup and continue cooking for a further 8 mins or until all ingredients are tender. Remove from heat, add grated cheese and stir until it just melts.

For babies under 6 mths, blend in an electric liquidizer, or put macaroni and vegetables through a sieve or hand blender, or mash with a fork, before returning to the liquid and reheating, without boiling.

Ways with Eggs

Eggs are included in combination with other foods in every section of this book, as they are an excellent source of nourishment for babies, but here are a few straightforward ways of serving them, more or less on their own.

Coddled Egg

1 egg   dash vinegar

Bring the egg to the boil covered with cold water and a dash of vinegar (to help prevent the shell from cracking) then remove from the heat. Leave the egg in the hot water, covered with a lid, to cook for a further 7 mins for soft boiled, and 20 mins for hard-boiled. For babies under 8 mths it is probably better to offer the yolk only (mashed or sieved and mixed with a little baby milk if hard-boiled) as the white sometimes causes an allergic reaction in the very young.

For older babies this is the best way to give the white at first, as the slow, gentle cooking makes it more digestible.

Poached Egg

1 egg – yolk only for a baby under 8 mths

For babies under 8 mths, separate yolk from white by breaking the shell in half and allowing the white to run into a container (save for adult use) as you pass the yolk from one half of the shell to the other. Put the yolk in a cup. For older babies, break the whole egg into a cup.

Bring about 2 ins (6 cm) water to a simmer, stir it, and slide the egg or yolk from the cup into the gently swirling water. Cook with water just off the boil until the egg is set, 3–5 mins.

Remove with a draining spoon and serve mashed, chopped, as it is, or on toast, depending on the stage reached.

Scrambled Egg

dot butter
1 egg – yolk only for a baby
  under 8 mths

1 tbsp baby milk, or 2 tbsps if
  yolk only used
dash salt for babies over 8 mths

Melt butter over water in the top of a double saucepan. Mix egg with milk and salt, if used, and stir into butter. Cook, stirring occasionally, until just set and still soft. (This can also be cooked in a small heavy saucepan over a low heat.)

Serve alone or with toast.

Spinach Scramble

dot butter
1 egg – yolk only for a baby
  under 8 mths
1 tbsp baby milk, or 2 tbsps if
  yolk only used

1 dessertsp finely grated cheese
  (optional)
dash salt for babies over 8 mths
2–4 leaves spinach or 1–2 oz
  (about 30 g) frozen spinach

Scramble egg as above, stirring in cheese, if used, just as it sets.

If fresh, wash spinach well in a bowl, changing water once or twice. Cook in about ½ inch (1–2 cm) simmering water until tender, 10–15 mins. Cook frozen spinach according to instructions on packet.

For babies under 6 mths, put spinach through a hand blender and stir into egg.

For older babies, mash or chop spinach according to stage reached and serve scrambled egg on top of it.

Baked Egg

(for babies over 8 mths)

2 tomatoes	1 tbsp milk
1 egg	dash salt
1 heaped tbsp grated cheese (optional)	dot butter

Make a thick purée of the tomatoes, as in 'Purées Galore'. Break egg into a small casserole smeared with butter, sprinkle on cheese, if used, spoon over the tomato purée and milk, add salt and dot lightly with butter. Cover with foil and bake at 325°F (160°C), Gas 3, until the egg is just set, 20–25 mins.

Egg en Cocotte

Prepare exactly as for Baked Egg above but cook in a pan standing in simmering water half-way up the casserole for 20–30 mins, or until the egg is just set.

Cottage Bake

½ egg – yolk only for babies under 8 mths	1 oz (25 g) cottage cheese dot butter

Beat egg and stir into cheese (which is probably best sieved or put through a hand blender first for babies under 6 mths). Put into a small, lightly buttered casserole, cover with foil and bake at 350°F (180°C), Gas 4, or steam, until set, 15–20 mins.

French Toast

(for babies over 8 mths)

1 egg   1 slice brown bread
2 tbsps milk   dot butter
dash salt

Beat egg with milk and salt in a flat dish. Soak bread in the egg mixture. Melt enough butter to cover the bottom of the pan, but do not let it turn brown. Cook eggy bread in this, turning once, until golden on each side. Cut into cubes or fingers.

Egg Mornay

(for babies over 8 mths)

1 egg   2 dessertsps very hot milk or
1 oz (25 g) or about 2 tbsps   water
  finely grated mild Cheddar
  cheese

Poach egg. Put cheese through a hand blender, pour hot milk or water onto it and stir until smoothly blended. Mash or chop the egg and stir into the sauce, or leave the egg whole and pour sauce over it, according to your baby's taste.

Cheese Choice

Like eggs you will find cheese included in many recipes elsewhere in this book, as it is both nutritious and easy to include in small quantities.

In this section are a few cheesy specials that went down particularly well with our baby testers.

Baby Croquettes

1 teasp raw egg yolk

2 tbsps grated mild Cheddar cheese

3 tbsps freshly cooked and mashed, unsalted potato

dot butter

2–3 tbsps baby milk for babies under 8 mths

1 tbsp finely crushed cornflakes for babies over 8 mths

Mix raw egg and grated cheese with the mashed potato.

For babies under 8 mths, bake the mixture in a lightly buttered casserole covered with foil at 350°F (180°C), Gas 4, or steam, until set, and mash with a little heated milk if the consistency is not liquid enough.

For older babies, form potato mixture into cork-shaped croquettes and roll in the cornflake crumbs. Bake on a lightly buttered tin at 350°F (180°C), Gas 4, for 30 mins.

Mashed carrots, swede or turnip instead of potato make very good croquettes too.

Cheese Custard

1 egg – yolk only for babies
    under 8 mths
1 tbsp grated mild Cheddar
    cheese

¼ pint (5 fl oz, 125 ml) baby
    milk
dot butter

Beat egg, add cheese, and stir in milk. Pour into a lightly buttered casserole, cover with foil, and bake at 350°F (180°C), Gas 4, or steam, until set, about 20 mins.

Cheese Fool

1 small eating apple or 3 tbsps
    thick cooked apple purée, or
    any other fruit purée from
    'Purées Galore'

2 tbsps cottage cheese

Peel finely, core and chop apple roughly. Whizz apple (or other puréed fruit) together with cheese in an electric blender until smooth.

Cheese Pudding

¼ pint (5 fl oz, 125 ml) baby
    milk
1 heaped tbsp brown
    breadcrumbs
1 egg – yolk only for babies
    under 8 mths

1 tbsp finely grated mild
    Cheddar cheese
dot butter

Boil milk, pour over breadcrumbs and leave to soak for a few mins. Add beaten egg and cheese. Mix well, turn into a lightly buttered casserole and cover with foil. Bake at 375°F (190°C), Gas 5, or steam, until set and risen, about 20 mins.

For babies under 6 mths, put through a hand blender and mix the pudding with a little baby milk if necessary, to give the right consistency.

Cheese Risotto

1 tomato
1 tbsp rice

1 heaped tbsp grated cheese
1-2 teasps baby milk (optional)

Peel, de-seed and chop tomato. Wash rice in a sieve under running cold water and simmer with the tomato and 4 tbsps water for 13 mins. Remove from heat, add cheese, stir and return to low heat, adding milk if used, until cheese melts into the rice mixture, but do not allow to re-boil.

For babies under 6 mths put through a hand blender.

Cheese and Tomato

1 tbsp cottage cheese

1 tomato

Make a thick purée of the tomato as in 'Purées Galore'.

For babies under 6 mths, sieve or put cheese through a hand blender before mixing with the tomato purée.

Cheesy Baked Potato

1 potato without blemishes
1 tbsp cottage cheese or 1 tbsp
  grated Cheddar cheese

1-2 teasps baby milk

Wash and scrub potato well and bake at 400°F (200°C), Gas 6, until soft when gently squeezed, 45–60 mins. Sieve or put cottage cheese through a hand blender.

Cut cooked potato in half, scoop out the inside (leaving the jacket intact) and mash with the cheese and enough milk to make a fairly stiff consistency.

For babies not feeding themselves, serve as it is, mixing with a little heated milk if necessary.

For more advanced babies, return the mixture to the jacket, fork over the top and let them spoon it out themselves and chew at the jackets if they wish, provided you are there to avoid choking.

Ham in a Halo
(for babies over 8 mths)

2–3 oz (75 g) very lean ham   2 tbsps cottage cheese
2 tomatoes

If salty, soak ham in cold water for 3–5 hrs, then dice and simmer until tender, 12–15 mins. Drain. Peel, de-seed, and chop the tomatoes. Mix ham (chopped small or puréed) with tomatoes and serve inside a ring of cottage cheese.

Welsh Rarebit
(for babies over 8 mths)

1 teasp butter   1 tbsp milk
1 tbsp grated Cheddar cheese   ½ raw egg yolk

Over simmering water in the top of a double saucepan, melt the butter. Stir in the cheese, then the milk, a little at a time, and finally add the beaten egg yolk, still stirring. Continue stirring until the mixture becomes thick and creamy. Do not overcook.

Serve with rusks or on toast.

Vegetable Variety

Apart from accompanying meat or fish in traditional ways, vegetables also make marvellous little meals on their own, with the addition of cheese or egg.

Baby Bavarian Cabbage

1 small apple
1 slice onion for babies over
  8 mths
6 tbsps finely shredded white or
  red cabbage

3 tbsps water
½ teasp brown sugar
1 or 2 drops lemon juice
dash salt for babies over 8 mths

Wash, peel and chop apple very small. Finely chop onion. Mix all ingredients and simmer slowly, covered, for 1 hr.

For babies under 6 mths, put through a hand blender or sieve.

Creamed Cabbage

2 large or 3 medium leaves
  green cabbage
4 tbsps baby milk

dash salt for babies over 8 mths
1 teasp baby cereal

Wash cabbage well, shred finely, and put with milk and salt, if used, into a small, heavy pan. Simmer slowly, covered, until cabbage is cooked (when a fork will slide easily into the stalk parts). (If slight curdling appears, the heat is too great, but the edibility of the cabbage will be unaffected.)

Drain off the milky cooking liquid and mix enough of it with the baby cereal to make a thickish sauce. Add the cabbage.

For babies under 6 mths, put through a hand blender before serving.

Carrots and Cottage Cheese

1 carrot   1 tbsp cottage cheese

Peel and dice carrot and simmer in about 1 inch (3 cm) water, covered, until tender, 15–20 mins.

For babies under 6 mths, mash carrot finely, put cottage cheese through a hand blender, and mix.

For older babies, mix diced cooked carrot and crumbled cottage cheese.

Cauliflower Cheese

3 or 4 florets cauliflower   1–2 dessertsps baby milk or
1 dessertsp baby   water
  cereal   1 tbsp grated cheese

Wash cauliflower and simmer in about 1 inch (3 cm) water, covered, until tender, 7–10 mins. Drain, save liquid, and keep cauliflower warm. Mix the baby cereal with enough of the cooking liquid and the baby milk to make a thickish sauce. Bring it slowly to the boil, stir in the grated cheese, but do not allow to boil.

For babies under 6 mths, put cauliflower through a hand blender, mash finely with a fork, or sieve, and mix with the cheese sauce.

For older babies, roughly chop the cauliflower and stir into the cheese sauce.

Celery and Tomato Cheese

2 stalks celery
1 teasp baby cereal
1 dessertsp baby milk or water

1 tomato
1 tbsp grated cheese

Wash and chop celery and simmer in about an inch (3 cm) water, covered, until tender, 10–20 mins. Drain, saving liquid. Mix the baby cereal with enough of the cooking liquid and baby milk to make a sauce. Purée the tomato as on page 35, add to the sauce and heat gently, bringing to the boil. Remove from heat and stir in cheese.

For babies under 6 mths, put celery through a hand blender before adding to the sauce.

For older babies, chop or mash celery according to stage reached.

Cheese Mix

1 carrot
5 sprouts

1 dessertsp mild Cheddar cheese
1 dessertsp boiling water

Peel and slice carrot. Wash sprouts in salted water and remove any blemished outer leaves and stalks. Simmer together in about 1 inch (3 cm) water, covered, until both are tender.

While they are cooking, put the cheese through a hand blender and mix with the boiling water to make a sauce.

For babies under 6 mths, put sprouts through a hand blender, mash carrot finely and mix, adding cheese sauce, with a little of the cooking liquid, if necessary, to give the right consistency.

For older babies, mash carrots and sprouts and mix with the cheese sauce.

Courgette with Tomato and Cheese

1 courgette   1 dessertsp grated mild
1 tomato   Cheddar cheese

Prepare and cook courgette as in 'Purées Galore', page 31; mash for babies under 6 mths, leave sliced for older babies. Make a thickish purée of the tomato as in 'Purées Galore', page 35. Stir together over a gentle heat with the cheese until it melts. Do not allow to boil.

Eggy Carrot

1 carrot $\frac{1}{2}$ hard-boiled egg yolk

Peel and slice carrot and simmer in about 1 inch (3 cm) water, covered, until tender, 15–20 mins. Drain and mash carrot finely. Mash or sieve egg yolk and mix with carrot.

Marrow Cheese

1 slice marrow – about 1 in   few drops vegetable oil
    (3 cm) thick   1 dessertsp cornflakes, finely
1 teasp egg yolk   crushed
1 tbsp grated cheese

Peel, remove seeds and pith, and cube marrow. Simmer in about 1 inch (3 cm) water, covered, until soft, about 15 mins. Drain well and mash with a fork. Stir in beaten egg yolk and cheese, then turn into a lightly oiled casserole. Sprinkle with the cornflake crumbs, cover with foil, and bake at 350°F (180°C), Gas 4, or steam, for 20 mins.

Potato Casserole

1 potato	dot butter
2 tomatoes	1 tbsp baby milk
1 tbsp grated cheese	

Wash, scrub, peel and thinly slice potato. Peel, de-seed and chop tomato. Put potato, tomato and cheese in layers in a lightly buttered casserole, finishing with the tomato. Spoon milk over, cover with foil, and bake at 375°F (190°C), Gas 5, or steam, until potatoes are cooked, about 30 mins.

For babies under 6 mths, mash or put through a hand blender.

Potato Pudding

1 egg yolk	1 potato
5 tbsps baby milk	dash salt for babies over 8 mths
1 slice onion for babies over 8 mths	few drops vegetable oil

Beat egg yolk and milk together. Grate onion, if used. Scrub, peel and grate potato. Mix potato, onion, salt if used, and egg with milk and turn into an oiled casserole. Cover with foil, and bake at 350°F (180°C), Gas 4, or steam, until set and cooked, about 1 hr.

Sprouts with Cheese Sauce

5 brussels sprouts	1–2 dessertsps baby milk or water
1 dessertsp baby cereal	1 tbsp grated Cheddar cheese

Wash sprouts in salted water and remove blemished outer leaves and stalks. Simmer in about 1 inch (3 cm) water, covered, until tender, 7–12 mins. Mix the baby cereal with enough of the cooking liquid and baby milk to make a thickish sauce. Bring to the boil slowly, remove from heat and add cheese.

For babies under 6 mths, put sprouts through a hand blender before adding to the sauce.

For older babies, mash or chop sprouts according to the stage reached, before stirring into the sauce.

Tomatoes au Gratin

3 tomatoes
1 slice onion for babies over 8 mths
few drops vegetable oil

1 tbsp finely grated Cheddar cheese
1 tbsp brown breadcrumbs

Peel, de-seed and chop tomatoes. Chop onion very finely or grate, if used. Into a small, lightly oiled casserole put tomato sprinkled with onion, cheese and breadcrumbs in layers, finishing with the crumbs. Cover with foil and bake at 350°F (180°C), Gas 4, or steam, for 30 mins.

For babies under 6 mths, put through a hand blender and mix with a little baby milk, if necessary, to give the right consistency.

Vegetable Mould

1 carrot and 1 small parsnip or an equivalent quantity of any other vegetables from 'Purées Galore'

dash salt for babies over 8 mths
2 teasps raw egg yolk
2 teasps grated Cheddar cheese
few drops vegetable oil

Peel and slice carrot and parsnip. Simmer together in about 1 inch (3 cm) water, covered, with salt if used, until tender. Drain, mash and mix with egg and cheese. Spoon mixture into a lightly oiled heatproof mould, cover with foil and bake at 350°F (180°C), Gas 4, or steam until firm, 20–30 mins. Leave to cool for a few mins and turn out of mould.

For babies under 6 mths, mash with a little heated baby milk or water if it is too thick.

For older babies, cut up for spoon or finger feeding.

Vegetables and Gravy

2 tbsps any vegetables from   1 tbsp of stock (see
  'Purées Galore', freshly   'Small Stocks',
  cooked without salt   page 64)

For babies under 6 mths, put vegetable(s) through a hand
blender (mash or chop for older babies) and add to stock. Reheat
all together, bringing to the boil, before serving.

Vegetable Timbale

1 egg yolk   few drops vegetable oil
4 tbsps baby milk
½ cup freshly cooked, diced
  vegetables (no salt) – potato,
  carrot, peas, beans or any
  others from 'Purées Galore'

Beat egg yolk with milk and add vegetables, puréed for babies
under 6 mths. Turn into a lightly oiled casserole. Cover with foil
and bake at 350°F (180°C), Gas 4, or steam, until set, about
30 mins. To test, insert a knife blade, which will come out clean
when the timbale is cooked.

Scrumptious Puddings

Fresh fruit is the best dessert for a baby, but if she has a weakness for sweet things, it is better to give her puddings than sweets between meals. It means that you can control the sweetness and be sure that the ingredients, other than sugar, are wholesome – fresh fruit, milk, eggs and so on. Anyway, here are a few scrumptious puddings to try.

Apple Brown Betty

1 small cooking apple
1–2 teasps sugar
2 tbsps brown breadcrumbs
3 tbsps water
dot margarine

Wash, peel, core and thinly slice apple. Lightly grease a small casserole and put in apples, sugar and breadcrumbs in layers, finishing with the crumbs. Spoon water over, dot lightly with margarine and cover with foil. Bake at 350°F (180°C), Gas 4, or steam, until apples are tender, about 45 mins.

For babies under 6 mths, put pudding through a hand blender before serving.

Apple Mousse

1 small apple, cooking or eating
2–3 tbsps water
1–2 teasps sugar if cooking apple is used
½ egg yolk
drop lemon juice
1 tbsp natural, unsweetened yogurt (optional)

Prepare, cook, if necessary, and purée apple as in 'Purées

Galore'. Beat egg yolk into the apple purée, add lemon juice and bring the mixture to the boil slowly, stirring. Remove from heat. Stir in yogurt, if using.

(Puréed apricots, banana, peach, pear, plum, prune or melon make delicious mousses too.)

Baked Egg Custard

1 egg yolk
8 tbsps (5 fl oz, ¼ pint, 125 ml) baby milk

½ teasp sugar

Beat the egg yolk with the sugar and add the milk. Pour into a small casserole, cover with foil, and bake at 325°F (160°C), Gas 3, or steam, until set (a knife will come out clean when inserted).

Baked Trifle

6 plums or prunes or an equivalent quantity of any other fruit from 'Purées Galore'
1 sponge finger or piece of sponge cake

½ egg – yolk only for babies under 8 mths
½ teasp sugar
4 tbsps (2½ fl oz, ⅛ pint, 60 ml) baby milk

Prepare, cook, if necessary, and purée fruit as in 'Purées Galore'. Spread fruit purée over the bottom of a small casserole. Cover with slices of sponge. Beat the egg and sugar together, stir in the milk and pour over the sponge and fruit purée. Cover with foil and bake at 325°F (160°C), Gas 3, or steam, until set, 25–30 mins.

Banana and Prunes

3 prunes
½ banana

1–2 drops lemon juice

Prepare, cook and purée prunes as in 'Purées Galore'. Mash banana and mix with prunes and lemon juice.

Blackcurrant Banana Dessert

⅓ banana
1 teasp blackcurrant drink or
    1 teasp blackcurrant purée
    made as in 'Purées Galore'

Mash banana and mix with the blackcurrant drink or purée.

Chocolate Pudding

1 egg – yolk only for babies
    under 8 mths
1 teasp cocoa powder

1 teasp sugar
1 cup baby milk

Beat the egg well. Make a cup of hot cocoa by mixing the cocoa powder and sugar with a little of the milk to a smooth paste, boil the rest of the milk and pour slowly onto the cocoa paste, stirring. Pour this hot cocoa slowly onto the beaten egg, stirring, and bake in a small casserole at 325°F (160°C), Gas 3, or steam, covered with foil, until set, 25–30 mins. Do not overcook.

(This chocolate custard is a very good way of getting toddlers who will not eat eggs in more obvious forms to devour them avidly.)

Custard Sauce

1 egg yolk
½ teasp sugar

7 tbsps (4 fl oz, 100 ml) baby
milk

Beat egg and sugar together and add milk. Stir over simmering water in a basin or in the top of a double saucepan, until it thickens. Remove from heat before it boils to avoid curdling. Serve on its own, with jelly, or with any of the fruits in 'Purées Galore'.

Fruit Jelly

1 level teasp gelatine
4 tbsps water and 4 tbsps
    undiluted blackcurrant drink
    or 8 tbsps puréed fruit from
    'Purées Galore'

Dissolve gelatine in 3 tbsps water over a gentle heat, stirring.
Remove from heat and stir in 1 tbsp water and 4 tbsps undiluted
blackcurrant drink or the 8 tbsps puréed fruit. Refrigerate until
set, 4–5 hrs.

Lemon Egg Jelly

¼ tablet lemon jelly
    (3 squares)
8 tbsps (5 fl oz, ¼ pint, 125 ml)
    water

1 egg – yolk only for babies
    under 8 mths
juice of ½ lemon or a few drops
    bottled pure lemon juice

Dissolve the jelly in the water by bringing slowly to the boil.
Beat the egg, stir in the lemon juice and the hot jelly liquid a
little at a time. Pour back into the pan and reheat for a few mins
without boiling. Pour into a mould, cool, and refrigerate until
set, 2–3 hrs.

Milk Jelly

¼ tablet jelly (3 squares) –
    raspberry, strawberry,
    blackcurrant or another
    flavour

2 tbsps (1 fl oz, 25 ml) water
7 tbsps (4 fl oz, 100 ml) baby
    milk

Dissolve the jelly by bringing it slowly to the boil in the water.
Leave to cool for 10 mins, then stir in milk, a little at a time.
Refrigerate until set, about 1 hr.

Orange and Honey Bread Pudding

8 tbsps (5 fl oz, ¼ pint, 125 ml)
  baby milk
½ teasp honey
1 heaped tbsp breadcrumbs

½ egg yolk
2 tbsps orange purée, page 38,
  or 2 tbsps fresh orange juice
dot margarine

Bring milk to the boil, stir in honey, pour over breadcrumbs and leave to soak for a few mins. Beat egg and add with orange purée or juice to the bread and milk. Turn into a lightly greased casserole, cover with foil, and bake at 350°F (180°C), Gas 4, or steam, until set, 30–35 mins.

Orange (or Lemon) Custard

1 egg yolk
½ teasp sugar (more if lemon
  juice is used)
2 tbsps fresh orange or lemon
  juice

8 tbsps (5 fl oz, ¼ pint, 125 ml)
  baby milk

Make as for Baked Egg Custard, page 86, mixing orange or lemon juice with beaten egg before adding the milk.

Pears and Chocolate Sauce

2 teasps baby rice
7 teasps baby milk
3 heaped teasps grated
  chocolate

1 soft ripe pear

Mix the baby rice with the milk and chocolate and bring to the boil slowly, stirring. Remove from heat. Peel, core and dice or mash the pear and stir into the sauce.

Rice Flummery

1 tbsp pudding rice	1 small egg yolk
8 tbsps (5 fl oz, ¼ pint, 125 ml) baby milk	½ teasp sugar

Wash rice in sieve under cold tap and cook with the milk in a bowl, or in the top of a double saucepan, over simmering water, until rice is tender, 25–30 mins. Remove from heat. Beat egg with sugar and add rice and milk slowly, stirring. Reheat, stirring, until the pudding thickens, 3–4 mins.

For babies under 6 mths, put through a hand blender.

Irresistible Ices

By no means all babies like ices – they are sometimes three or four years old before they are ready to enjoy the sudden coldness of them. These recipes are not suitable for very young babies, as you will see.

However as most older children, as well as many adults, find them irresistible, here are a few that we have found delicious. For practical reasons many of the recipes are given in family quantities. All will keep in the freezing compartment of a refrigerator for a day or two.

Chocolate Ice Cream
(for babies over 8 mths)

1 12 oz (325 g) tin evaporated milk
1 level teasp gelatine
5 tbsps boiling water

3 tbsps (1½ oz, 40 g) cocoa powder and 3 tbsps sugar or
5 tbsps (3 oz, 75 g) drinking chocolate powder
1 teasp vanilla essence

Boil the unopened tin of evaporated milk, covered with water, for 15 mins. Cool and chill in the refrigerator overnight.

Turn refrigerator to lowest setting. Whisk chilled evaporated milk until light and fluffy.

Dissolve the gelatine in 2 tbsps boiling water over a gentle heat, stirring. Slowly whisk the gelatine into the fluffy milk. Put into the freezing compartment until half frozen, 1–2 hrs.

Meantime, dissolve cocoa and sugar, or drinking chocolate

powder, in 3 tbsps boiling water and leave to cool. Chill mixer bowl by filling with iced water or putting in the refrigerator. Whisk the half-frozen milk in the cold bowl until fluffy again, add the cooled chocolate mixture and vanilla essence. Refreeze until firm, then return refrigerator setting to normal.

Honey Ice Cream

(for babies over 8 mths)

1 12 oz (325 g) tin evaporated milk	1 teasp vanilla essence
	2 eggs
2 tbsps water	3 tbsps runny honey
1 level teasp gelatine	

Boil the unopened tin of evaporated milk, covered with water, for 15 mins. Cool and chill in the refrigerator overnight.

Turn refrigerator to lowest setting. Whisk chilled milk, preferably in an electric mixer bowl at fast speed, until light and fluffy (when whisk leaves a trail).

Dissolve gelatine in the water, bringing to the boil slowly, stirring. Into the fluffy evaporated milk slowly whisk the dissolved gelatine, the vanilla essence, the egg yolks and honey. Place in the refrigerator ice compartment until half frozen, 1 hr or more.

Chill the mixer bowl by filling with iced water or putting in the refrigerator. Just before taking out the half-frozen ice cream, whisk the egg whites to soft peak stage.

Whisk the ice cream in the cold mixer bowl for about 30 secs, then gently fold in the egg whites.

Refreeze until firm, then return refrigerator setting to normal.

Lemon Ice Cream

(for babies over 8 mths)

½ pint (10 fl oz, 250 ml)   5 oz (125 g) icing sugar
  evaporated milk   4 lemons
2 eggs

Boil unopened tin of evaporated milk, covered with water, for 15 mins. Cool and chill in the refrigerator overnight.

Turn refrigerator to coldest setting. Whisk the egg yolks and sugar until thick and creamy, preferably with an electric mixer. Stir in finely grated rind and juice of the lemons.

Whisk the chilled evaporated milk until light and fluffy, mix half of it with the egg yolk and lemon mixture; refrigerate the other half for the time being. Put the lemon and milk mixture into the freezing compartment until half frozen, 2–3 hrs.

Chill the mixer bowl by filling with iced water or putting in the refrigerator. Whisk the egg whites to soft peak stage.

Whisk the half-frozen lemon and milk in the cold bowl until smooth, then with a large metal spoon fold in the rest of the fluffed milk and the egg whites. Refreeze until firm, then turn refrigerator setting back to normal.

Prune Ice Cream

(for babies over 8 mths)

½ pint (10 fl oz, 250 ml)   1 dessertsp lemon juice
  evaporated milk   1 tbsp castor sugar
8 oz (225 g) dried prunes

Boil unopened tin of evaporated milk for 15 mins, covered with water. Cool and chill in the refrigerator overnight.

Wash and soak the prunes overnight. Simmer, well covered with water, until tender, 20–30 mins. Drain, cool and remove stones.

Turn refrigerator to coldest setting. Whizz prunes with 2–3 tbsps cooking liquid, the lemon juice and sugar in an electric liquidizer, or mash or sieve until puréed. Put prune mixture into the ice compartment until half frozen, 1–2 hrs. Whisk chilled evaporated milk until thick and fluffy just before removing half-frozen prunes. Cool mixer bowl by filling with iced water or putting into the refrigerator.

Whisk half-frozen prunes in the cold bowl until smooth and fold into the fluffy milk.

Refreeze until firm, then turn refrigerator back to normal setting. (Apricots, peaches or plums, instead of prunes, are extremely good in this ice cream too.)

Orange and Lemon Sorbet

(for babies over 8 mths)

1 orange	1 egg, white and yolk separated
1 lemon	1 tbsp sugar

With a sharp knife remove a thin peel, avoiding the pith, from the orange and lemon. Just cover with water and simmer the peel for 15 mins. Leave to cool, pour through a sieve, discard peel, and add liquid plus 4 tbsps water to the juice from the orange and the lemon. Beat egg yolk well with the sugar, add the juices, then put into the ice compartment until almost solid. Chill mixing bowl by filling with iced water or putting in the refrigerator, then whisk the half-frozen mixture in the cold bowl until smooth. Refreeze until almost solid again.

Whisk egg whites to soft peak stage just before taking out the frozen lemon and egg mixture, then roughly break up the mixture with a fork. Fold in the egg whites and refreeze until solid.

Blackcurrant Water Ice

(for babies over 8 mths)

6 tbsps water   1 egg white
6 tbsps blackcurrant drink

Mix the water and blackcurrant liquid. Whisk the egg white to
the soft peak stage and fold it into the blackcurrant juice as well
as you can (they will mix better after being half frozen). Put the
mixture into the ice compartment until partly frozen, about 1 hr.
Turn mixture over lightly with a fork, mashing a little, until the
ice crystals are broken up and thoroughly mixed with the foamy
parts. Refreeze until set.

Lemon Water Ice

(for babies over 8 mths)

1 dessertsp sugar   3 tbsps pure lemon juice
8 tbsps (¼ pint, 5 fl oz, 125 ml)   finely grated rind of ½ lemon
  water   1 egg white

Turn refrigerator to lowest setting. Boil the sugar and water
together for 10 mins. Remove from heat and leave to cool, then
add lemon rind and juice. Put in the freezer compartment until
it is half frozen and mushy.

Whisk egg white to the soft peak stage. Break up the ice
crystals in the half-frozen lemon mixture with a fork, and fold
in the egg white with a large metal spoon.

Refreeze until firm, then turn refrigerator back to normal
setting.

Iced Fruit Yogurt

(for babies over 8 mths)

½ cup natural, unsweetened
   yogurt
1 cup puréed fruit (see 'Purées
   Galore')

honey (runny variety) to
   sweeten, if necessary
1 egg white

Half freeze the yogurt in the ice compartment of the refrigerator, about 1 hr, and combine it with the puréed fruit and honey, if used. Refreeze to half-frozen state about 1 hr.

Whisk egg white to soft peak stage. Break up any ice crystals that have formed in the half-frozen yogurt and fruit mixture with a fork, and fold in the egg white with a large metal spoon. Refreeze until firm.

Finger Foods
and Teatime Titbits

At about six or seven months your baby will suddenly want to chew, and to feed herself. It is very important to give her the opportunity to develop both of these skills, as soon as she is ready. Fingers are the forerunners for spoons, so let her have a go, no matter what the mess at first. But constant supervision is essential – it is so easy for a baby to choke on a piece of lumpy food before she has learnt to chew it soft and small enough to swallow comfortably.

Vegetables

Cooked

Dice or chop small any of the following vegetables:

aubergine	haricot beans
beetroot (if you can face the stains)	marrow
	parsnip
broad beans	peas
butter beans	potato
cabbage, both leaf and tender stalk	sprouts
	swede
carrot	sweet peppers, green or red
cauliflower	tomato, skinned and de-seeded
celery	(uncooked)
courgette	turnip
French or runner beans	

Vegetable and Egg Dice

2 tbsps any thick vegetable   1 hard-boiled egg yolk
   purée from 'Purées Galore'

Mash or sieve the egg yolk and mix with the vegetable purée.
Press flat in a shallow container with a fork or a spoon and cut
into small dice.

Try also Vegetable Mould, page 83, and Baked Lentil Roast,
Butter Bean Loaf, Nut Roast, Soya Bean Loaf, Vegetable
Protein Loaf, pages 105, 106, 109, 111 and 114.

Raw

Once your baby has got used to finger feeding himself with soft
cooked, diced vegetables, try giving him any of the following
raw, well-cleaned, either finely grated or in sticks or cubes to
bite on, under your constant supervision, of course, to avoid the
possibility of choking:

cabbage, white, red or green   marrow
carrot   parsnip
cauliflower   swede
celery   sweet pepper, green or red
lettuce   turnip

When teething, sticks or cubes of vegetables such as carrot,
swede, turnip or parsnip, chilled for a few minutes in iced water,
can be wonderfully soothing for inflamed gums.

Fruits

Dice or chop any of the following, well-washed if served uncooked:

apple, cooked at first, then peeled, cored and quartered

apricots, fresh ripe, peeled and de-stoned; or cooked, dried apricots

banana, sliced

cherries, peeled at first, and de-stoned

figs, cooked and de-seeded at first

grapes, peeled, de-seeded, halved or quartered

melon, soft ripe, peeled cubes

orange, peeled, de-pipped and segmented or diced

peaches, ripe, peeled and de-stoned

pear, raw ripe William or similar, peeled, cored and quartered

plums, peeled at first and de-stoned

prunes, cooked and de-stoned

raisins, seedless, soaked and cooked at first

sultanas, soaked and cooked at first

Meat and Fish

Well-cooked, lean, tender pieces (about the size of a pea to begin with) or any of the following meats make good first finger foods, prepared and cooked as in 'Purées Galore':

bacon, lean, grilled slowly until tender and well-cooked

beef

brains

chicken

ham, lean (boiled)

heart

kidney

lamb

liver

lean pork (well-cooked)

sweetbreads

turkey

Also Kidney and Beef Pâté, page 52, or Liver and Beef Pâté, page 54.

Pasta Pick-up

2–3 tbsps freshly cooked
macaroni or other small
pasta

2–3 tbsps diced, freshly cooked,
lean meat, liver or kidney

2 tbsps freshly cooked, diced
carrot or other colourful
vegetable

1 tomato, peeled, de-seeded and
quartered

Combine all ingredients by folding together lightly. Reheat over simmering water in a basin, or in the top of a double saucepan, if necessary, just before serving.

Any freshly cooked, white filleted fish like cod, halibut, haddock, coley, sole or plaice, that separates easily into flakes, is easy for small fingers to manage, after being carefully checked for stray bones. Small pieces of fresh or tinned, drained salmon or tuna are also suitable.

See also the following recipes: Fish Patty, Fish Mould, or Mini Fish Cakes, pages 61–2.

Eggs and Cheese

Hard-boiled, or well-poached eggs, quartered or cut smaller, yolk only for babies up to 8 mths.

Give mild Cheddar cheese at first, grated or diced small, or cottage cheese, crumbled.

Cheese, Apple and Tomato

Mix either grated hard cheese or crumbled cottage cheese with grated or diced apple and tomato, peeled, de-seeded and chopped.

Cheese Toasts

Toast one side of a slice of bread. Lightly butter or margarine the other side and cover with grated or thinly sliced Cheddar cheese. Put under the grill until the cheese has just melted. Cut into cubes or fingers.

Other cheese recipes are Cottage Bake, page 72, and Baby Croquettes, Cheese Pudding, Cheesy Baked Potato or Welsh Rarebit, pages 74–7.

Rusks

Plain Rusks

½-inch (1–2 cm) thick slices white or brown bread

Cut into neat fingers and place on a baking tray, covered by another heavy baking tray or tin, to give rusks a smooth surface.

Bake at 275°F (140°C), Gas 1, until crisp right through, about 30 mins, turning once half-way to brown both sides lightly.

Stored in an airtight container, they will keep for a week or two.

Cheese Rusks

1 oz (25 g) mild Cheddar cheese   ½ inch thick slice bread
3 tbsps boiling water

Put cheese through a hand blender and mix with boiling water, 1 tbsp at a time. Cut bread into neat cubes and dip both sides in the cheesy liquid. Bake on a well-greased, shallow baking tin at 275°F (140°C), Gas 1, until crisp right through, about 30 mins, turning half-way through so that each side becomes lightly browned.

Stored in an airtight container, they will keep for a few days.

You will find recipes for Nutritious Teething Rusks and Savoury Sesame Biscuits on pages 109 and 111.

Sandwiches

Make first offerings postage-stamp size, with thinly sliced bread smeared with butter. Use white or one of the brown breads, and vary it from day to day.

Suggested Fillings

Cheese: Cheddar, Edam, Gouda or any other mild hard cheese thinly sliced; finely grated and beaten with a little butter or margarine; or put through a hand blender and mixed to a thick paste with boiling water (1 oz, 25 g, cheese to 1 tbsp water).

Cheese, as above, or cottage cheese, mixed with thick tomato, carrot or fruit purée from 'Purées Galore'.

Cheese and cucumber.

Cheese and Marmite.

Cheese and a smear of honey.

Eggs: hard-boiled and mashed with a dash of salt, a dot of butter or margarine and a few drops of baby milk.

Egg and Marmite.

Egg and tomato, peeled, de-seeded and chopped, or thickly puréed.

Fruit: puréed thickly, chopped or mashed – apples, apricots, bananas, blackcurrants, dates, figs, prunes, seedless raisins or sultanas.

Banana and date.

Apple and prune.

Apple, grated, with honey.

Peanut butter.

Lemon Curd

(for babies over 8 mths)

rind and juice of 2 lemons	8 oz (225 g) sugar
3 eggs	2 oz (50 g) butter or margarine

Grate lemon rind finely. Squeeze juice from lemons and strain it. Beat eggs, add rind, juice, sugar and butter, and cook over simmering water in a basin or in the top of a double saucepan, stirring, until it thickens. Test by dropping a little into cold water to see if it sets when cool.

Pour into hot, sterilized containers and seal while hot.

Meat : beef, chicken, ham or liver spreads. Make as for purées, beating with a little butter or margarine instead of cooking liquid to give a spreading consistency.

Beef and tomato, peeled, de-seeded and chopped or thickly puréed.

Chicken and ham.

Ham and apple, grated.

Fish : salmon, tuna or sardines. Drain off liquid after opening tin and mash. Use alone or with tomato, curd or cottage cheese.

Meatless Baby Fare

Your baby doesn't have to be a vegetarian to enjoy the recipes in this section. The ingredients used are both nutritious and very economical compared with meat or fish, and soya beans (and flour made from these) and nuts have a protein content as high as beef. These and other pulses – beans, peas and lentils – can be prepared in many appetizing ways too.

All these recipes went down particularly well with our two young testers, neither of whom is being brought up as a vegetarian, nor had they tried dishes of this kind before.

Baked Bean Quickie

2 tbsps baked beans from a tin	1 dessertsp wholemeal
1 tbsp grated Cheddar cheese	breadcrumbs
1 teasp egg yolk	few drops vegetable oil

Mash beans with a fork or put through a hand blender and add grated cheese, egg yolk and breadcrumbs. Mix well. Turn into a small lightly oiled casserole, cover with foil, and bake at 350°F (180°C), Gas 4, or steam, for 30 mins.

For babies under 6 mths, mash or put the mixture through a hand blender and mix with a little of the tomato liquid from the tin, or baby milk, to give a smooth consistency.

Baked Lentil Roast

1 teasp egg yolk
2 tbsps lentils, puréed as in
'Purées Galore'
1 teasp finely grated cheese

1 dessertsp breadcrumbs
dot yeast extract
few drops vegetable oil

Beat egg yolk and mix it with the other ingredients. Spoon the mixture into a small oiled heatproof dish, cover with foil and bake at 350°F (180°C), Gas 4, or steam for 30–40 mins until set.

Black-eyed Bean Stew

2 tbsps uncooked, or 5 tbsps
cooked, black-eyed beans
1 small carrot
½ parsnip
1 small stalk celery

1 slice onion for babies over
8 mths
1–2 teasps baby cereal for
babies over 8 mths
dash salt for babies over 8 mths

If uncooked, wash beans, soak overnight and simmer, covered with fresh water and a lid, until tender, about 50 mins.

Clean, peel and dice the carrot and parsnip. Clean and chop celery and chop onion finely, if used.

Simmer all the ingredients, including the cooked beans, and salt if used, with about 6 tbsps (4 fl oz, 100 ml) water, covered, for 30 mins.

For babies under 6 mths, put through a hand blender, mixing with enough of the cooking liquid to give a smooth consistency.

For older babies, mix a little of the cooking liquid with the baby cereal, stir it into the stew and reheat for 1–2 mins.

Brown Rice and Cheese

(for babies over 8 mths)

2 tbsps uncooked, or 4 tbsps cooked, brown rice	2 tomatoes
1 slice onion for babies over 8 mths	dot butter
	dot yeast extract or Marmite
1 small carrot	1 tbsp grated Cheddar cheese

If rice is uncooked, wash and simmer until tender, 45–60 mins.

Chop onion finely, if used, clean, peel and dice carrot, peel, de-seed and chop tomatoes. Melt butter in a pan and gently toss onion in it until soft. Add carrot and tomatoes and simmer, covered, in about 1 inch (3 cm) water until tender, about 15 mins. Stir in yeast extract and rice and simmer for a further 5 mins. Drain off surplus liquid and stir in cheese over a low heat.

(White long grain rice, which is cooked by washing, and simmering for only 13 mins, could replace the brown rice, but it is not quite as nutritious.)

Butter Bean Loaf

2 tbsps dried, or 5 tbsps cooked, butter beans	1½ tbsps tomato purée
dot Marmite or yeast extract	1 tbsp crushed cornflakes
½ egg – yolk only for babies under 8 mths	few drops vegetable oil

If uncooked, soak butter beans overnight and simmer, covered, until very tender, 50–60 mins. Drain, saving liquid.

Mash beans with a fork and mix in the Marmite, egg, tomato purée, crushed cornflakes and 1–2 tbsps of the cooking liquid. Turn into a lightly oiled casserole. Bake, covered with foil, at 350°F (180°C), Gas 4, or steam, for 30 mins.

For babies under 6 mths, mix with a little of the butter bean cooking liquid if necessary, to obtain a soft enough consistency.

Cauliflower and Lentils

1 tbsp lentils	4 tbsps baby milk
2 or 3 sprigs cauliflower	1 tbsp grated Cheddar cheese
4 tbsps water	(optional)

Wash and soak lentils for an hour or so in boiling water. Wash cauliflower, break up the sprigs, and simmer with the soaked lentils, water and milk, very slowly (half-covered with a lid) until the cauliflower is tender, 20–30 mins.

For babies under 6 mths, mash lentils and cauliflower finely together, or put through a hand blender, adding enough of the cooking liquid to give a smooth consistency.

For older babies, mash or chop cauliflower according to stage reached. If cheese is used, put it through a hand blender, mix with 2 tbsps of the hot, milky cooking liquid, and stir into the cauliflower and lentil mixture. Serve with peas or green beans.

Chick Pea Stew

2 tbsps dry, or 5 tbsps cooked, chick peas	1 small carrot
1 small apple	1 teasp orange juice
	few drops soy sauce

If chick peas are uncooked, soak overnight and simmer until tender, 1 hr or more.

Clean, peel, core and dice apple and carrot.

Simmer all ingredients together with enough water to almost cover, for 20 mins, with the lid on the pan.

For babies under 6 mths, drain and put through a hand blender, adding enough of the cooking liquid to give a smooth consistency.

For older babies, serve with a little of the cooking liquid as a sauce, and cabbage, or tomatoes, peeled, de-seeded and chopped.

Haricot Bean Stew

2 tbsps uncooked, or 5 tbsps cooked, haricot beans	2 tomatoes
1 slice onion for babies over 8 mths	1 small carrot
	1 teasp vegetable oil
	dash salt for babies over 8 mths

If uncooked, soak beans overnight and simmer until tender, 45–50 mins.

Chop onion finely, if used. Clean, peel and dice carrot. Peel, de-seed and chop tomatoes. Heat oil in a pan and toss onion lightly in this until soft. Add carrot, tomatoes, cooked beans and salt, if used. Simmer, just covered with water and with a lid, until carrot is tender, about 20 mins.

For babies under 6 mths, put through a hand blender and mix with a little of the cooking liquid.

For older babies, mash or not, according to stage reached and serve with spinach or another green vegetable.

Lentil Cheese

2 tbsps lentils	dot Marmite or yeast extract
7 tbsps water	1 tbsp finely grated Cheddar cheese
dot butter	

Make a purée of the lentils by washing, and simmering slowly in the water until soft, about 30 mins. Press through a sieve and add 1–2 teasps water if too stiff.

Over a low heat, melt the butter in a pan and add lentil purée, yeast extract and cheese, stirring until cheese melts, but do not allow to boil.

Spoon feed it warm to your baby, or leave it to cool and use as a spread on bread or toast.

Nut Roast

(for babies over 8 mths)

1 tomato
1 slice onion
dot margarine
dot yeast extract
½ egg yolk
2 tbsps finely milled nuts
(liquidize or put through
hand blender)

3 tbsps wholemeal breadcrumbs
dash nutmeg
few drops vegetable oil

Chop onion finely and peel, de-seed and chop tomato. Simmer onion and tomato, just covered with water and a lid, until the onion is soft, 10–15 mins. Remove from heat and stir in the margarine, yeast extract, beaten egg, nuts, breadcrumbs and nutmeg, mixing well. Spoon the mixture into a lightly oiled casserole, cover with foil and bake at 350°F (180°C), Gas 4, or steam, until risen and set, about 45 mins.

Nutritious Teething Rusks

2 tbsps runny honey
1 tbsp black treacle
2 tbsps vegetable oil
1 egg yolk, beaten

8 tbsps wholewheat flour
8 tbsps soya flour
4 tbsps wheatgerm
1–4 tbsps baby milk

Beat honey, treacle, oil and egg yolk together. Mix flours and wheatgerm thoroughly and stir into the honey mixture, adding enough milk to make a stiff dough. Roll out on a board, sprinkled with wholewheat flour, to ¼ inch (½ cm) thickness, and cut into fingers. Bake on a lightly oiled tray at 350°F (180°C), Gas 4, for 15–20 mins, until crisp when cool. (Cool one quickly to test, to avoid burning.) These rusks are not very sweet; they will keep for a week or two in an airtight container.

Peanut Butter and Apple

1 small apple   1 level dessertsp peanut butter

Peel finely (the Vitamin C is just under the skin) and core apple, then grate it. Put it through a hand blender or liquidize it with a dessertsp of water. Stir apple into the peanut butter. Spoon feed it or serve spread on bread.

Red Bean Stew

(for babies over 8 mths)

1 tbsp uncooked red kidney   1 slice onion
  beans   dash basil
1 small carrot   dash salt
½ parsnip   1 dessertsp baby rice
1 tomato

Soak beans overnight then, covered with water, bring to a fast boil for 20 minutes. Peel and dice carrot and parsnip, peel, de-seed and chop tomato, and chop onion finely. Simmer all ingredients except baby rice together, with ¼ pint water or more to cover well, until beans are tender, about 1 hr. Make a thickish sauce with the baby rice and 1–2 tbsps of the cooking liquid, add to the stew and reheat, stirring, before serving.

Savoury Cheese Curd

1 tbsp grated Cheddar cheese   1 tbsp soya bean curd (see
2 tbsps boiling water   recipe, page 111)
dot Marmite or yeast extract
  for babies over 8 mths

Put the cheese through a hand blender, mix with the boiling water, 1 tbsp at a time, and the Marmite, and stir into the curd.
  Serve with tomatoes, carrots or a green vegetable.

Savoury Sesame Biscuits

8 oz (225 g) wholewheat flour   dash salt for babies over 8 mths
2 oz (50 g) sesame seeds   8 tbsps vegetable oil
1 oz (25 g) soya flour   5–10 tbsps water

Mix flours, seeds and salt, if used. Pour in oil and blend well, then add enough water to make a stiff dough. Roll to about ¼ inch (½ cm) thick and cut into rounds or fingers.

Bake at 350°F (180°C), Gas 4, until crisp when cool, about 15–20 mins. (Cool one quickly to test, to avoid burning.)

Soya Cream Sauce

1 tbsp soya flour   1 tbsp water

Mix to a smooth paste and serve as it is or with any puréed or chopped vegetable or fruit – for suggestions see 'Purées Galore'.

(Very high in protein; our four-month-old tester loved it.)

Soya Bean Curd

2 tbsps uncooked soya beans

Wash beans, discard any extraneous bits and soak overnight. Simmer, well covered with water, and with a lid, until tender, 1–1½ hrs. (It is important to cook soya beans thoroughly.) Drain, saving the liquid.

Put the cooked soya beans with 8 tbsps of the cooking liquid in an electric liquidizer and whizz until the mixture is all smooth, stopping the machine and pushing the beans down towards the blades as necessary.

(As soya beans have a high protein content, this curd is very nutritious and can be added to soups, stews or baked moulds for extra nourishment.)

Soya Bean Loaf

2 tbsps uncooked or 4 tbsps
  cooked soya beans
1 tbsp baby milk
½ egg yolk
1 teasp grated onion for babies
  over 8 mths

dash salt for babies over 8 mths
2 tbsps wholemeal breadcrumbs
few drops vegetable oil

If uncooked, wash beans, discard any extraneous bits, soak overnight and simmer until tender, 1–1½ hrs (make sure they are well cooked).

Into an electric liquidizer put cooked beans, 8 tbsps water, 1 tbsp milk and the egg yolk. Whizz with onion and salt, if used, until mixed. Pour onto the breadcrumbs and mix together. Turn into a lightly oiled casserole, cover with foil, and bake at 350°F (180°C), Gas 4, or steam, for 20–30 mins until slightly risen.

For babies under 6 mths, put through a hand blender and mix with a little baby milk to give a smooth consistency. For older babies, serve with spinach or another green vegetable.

Soya Bean Stew

2 tbsps uncooked or 4 tbsps
  cooked soya beans
1 slice onion for babies over
  8 mths
1 stalk celery
dot butter
2 tbsps sweetcorn, tinned or
  frozen

2 tomatoes, puréed and made
  up to 4 tbsps liquid with
  tomato juice or water
1 tbsp grated Cheddar cheese
dot Marmite or yeast extract for
  babies over 8 mths

If uncooked, wash and discard any extraneous bits in the beans. Soak overnight and simmer until tender, and well cooked, 1–1½ hrs.

Chop onion finely, if used. Wash and chop celery. Melt butter in a small pan and soften onion in this. Add the beans, corn, tomato purée liquid and celery, and simmer, covered, for 45 mins. Remove from the heat and stir in the cheese.

For babies under 6 mths, put through a hand blender, adding enough of the cooking liquid to give a smooth consistency.

For older babies, mash or not according to taste, and stir in a dot of Marmite or yeast extract just before serving.

Soya Curd and Fruit

1 tbsp soya bean curd, made as recipe on page 111
2 tbsps thickly puréed fruit (any from 'Purées Galore')

dot of honey

Mix well together and serve.

Soya Curd and Vegetables

1 tbsp soya bean curd, made as recipe on page 111
2 tbsps thickly puréed vegetable (any from 'Purées Galore')

dot Marmite or yeast extract for babies over 8 mths

Mix well together and serve.

Soya Nut Savoury

1 tbsp soya bean curd, made as above

1 tbsp finely milled nuts
1 tbsp tomato purée

Mix well together and serve.

Vegetable Protein Loaf

(for babies over 8 mths)

3 tbsps boiling water
1 tbsp minced soya-textured
  vegetable protein (TVP),
  ham or beef flavour
3 tbsps wholewheat
  breadcrumbs

¼ teasp finely chopped
  parsley
½ egg
few drops vegetable oil

Pour the boiling water over the textured protein, leave to stand for a few mins, then stir in the breadcrumbs, parsley and egg. Spoon into a lightly oiled casserole, cover with foil and bake at 350°F (180°C), Gas 4, or steam, for 40 mins.

Serve with tomatoes, peeled, de-seeded and chopped, or a green vegetable – peas go especially well with this.

Meals to Freeze

If you have a freezer, it is certainly worth cooking in bulk for your baby and freezing in meal-sized portions. But to avoid waste, do make a small helping first to make sure he likes whatever you are proposing to freeze.

Our recipes give details for freezing as well as cooking and at the end of the section there are a great many references to recipes elsewhere in this book that could be cooked in larger quantities, simply by multiplying the ingredients given, and frozen on the lines suggested here.

Rules for Freezing Baby Foods

1. Freeze only fresh foods in perfect condition.
2. Use only scrupulously clean equipment for preparation, cooking and storage.
3. Handle food as little as possible and keep it very clean.
4. Cool cooked foods quickly and freeze immediately.
5. Turn control to coldest setting 2–3 hrs before freezing and return to normal setting only when food is frozen solid.
6. Seal food for freezing in moisture-proof, vapour-proof materials – containers like plastic boxes, wax and foil containers, all with close fitting lids; or strong polythene bags (exclude air and seal with paper-covered wire twists).
7. Label every item frozen, giving name of food or recipe, date cooked, and storage life.

8. Thaw food thoroughly, with a minimum of delay, and heat to boiling or the heat that is normally reached at the end of cooking time.
9. Never refreeze foods.
10. Avoid freezing the following:

bananas
custards, as they tend to
    separate
eggs, if raw in their shells,
    hard-boiled or poached

fresh milk, which separates and
    will not re-constitute
tomatoes, unless puréed or in
    a cooked dish

Baby Soup Stock

beef or mutton bones fresh
    from a butcher or bones or a
    chicken or turkey carcass left
    from your own cooking

Turn freezer control to coldest setting.

Break up large bones; get butcher to do this with fresh bones. Simmer, covered with water and a lid, for 3–4 hrs.

Cool quickly by standing pan, still covered with lid, in cold or iced water. Skim off any fat on the surface and strain.

Pack in ice-cube trays or portion-size containers, leaving ½ inch (1 cm) head space under lid. Label with name, date and storage life.

Freeze immediately until solid. If packed in ice-cube trays, remove and re-pack in lidded plastic boxes, wax or foil cartons or strong polythene bags, sealed with paper-covered wire twists, so that you can take out as many as you need each time. Return freezer control to normal.

Store up to 2 mths.

Thaw by heating to boiling point in a basin over simmering water, or in the top of a double saucepan, or by using the stock cubes in a soup, making quite sure they dissolve completely and boil before serving.

Beef (and other meat) Purées

2 lb (1 kg) lean stewing beef
¼ teasp Marmite or yeast
 extract for babies over 8 mths

Turn freezer control to coldest setting.

Trim all fat off meat, cut into cubes, bring to the boil just covered with water and stir in Marmite, if used. Simmer, covered, until tender, about 1 hr. In an electric liquidizer whizz meat, about 8 oz (225 g or so) at a time, with enough of the cooking liquid (covering about ½–⅔ of the meat in the liquidizer) to make a smooth purée.

Cool quickly by returning to pan, covering with lid, and standing in cold or iced water. Skim off any surface fat.

Pack in portion-sized containers – lidded plastic boxes, wax or foil containers – leaving ½ inch (1 cm) space at the top for expansion, or in ice cube trays. Label with name of food, date and storage life.

Freeze immediately until solid and repack any in ice-cube trays into containers, as above, or in strong polythene bags, sealed with paper-covered wire twists. Return freezer control to normal.

Store up to 2 mths.

Thaw by plunging container into warm water to release block and heating over simmering water in a basin or in the top of a double saucepan, stirring if necessary to prevent sticking as you bring it to boiling point. (Lamb, chicken, fowl, turkey, ham, kidney, liver or tongue can be frozen in this way. See 'Purées Galore' for guide to preparation, cooking and puréeing.)

Fish Purée

2 lb (1 kg) filleted fish
¼ teasp salt for babies over
  8 mths

Turn freezer control to lowest setting.

Choose very fresh, or frozen, filleted cod, haddock, halibut, coley, plaice, sole or salmon. Wash and dry fish if fresh, sprinkle with salt, if used, and steam (use a covered basin over a pan of water if no steamer available), until cooked, when flakes will separate easily, 15–30 mins.

Remove skin, check carefully for stray bones, then put fish in an electric liquidizer, about 8 oz (225 g) at a time with cooking liquid or water to well cover the blades, and whizz to a smooth purée. (Stop liquidizer to push fish down onto blades as necessary.)

Cool, pack, freeze, store and thaw as for Beef Purée, above.

Carrots (and other vegetables)

2 lb (1 kg) carrots   ¼ pint (5 fl oz, 125 ml) water

Turn freezer control to coldest setting.

Wash, peel and slice carrots. Bring water to the boil, add carrots and simmer until just cooked, 10–15 mins. Drain, saving liquid. Leave sliced, or purée by mashing finely with a fork, or whizz in an electric blender with the cooking liquid until smooth.

Cool quickly by standing, covered, in iced water.

Pack in portion-sized containers – lidded plastic boxes, waxed or foil cartons, or in ice-cube trays. Leave ½ inch (1 cm) head space in each. Label with name of food, date and storage life.

Freeze immediately until solid and re-pack carrots that have been frozen in ice-cube trays. Return freezer setting to normal.

Store up to 6 mths.

Thaw by plunging container into warm water to release block and heat over simmering water in a basin or in the top of a double saucepan, stirring if necessary to prevent sticking as you bring it to boiling point. Stir in egg yolk or 1–2 tbsps grated Cheddar cheese for a complete baby meal, but do not allow to re-boil.

(Other vegetables from 'Purées Galore' can be frozen in this way including parsnip, swedes, turnips, cauliflower, courgettes, tomatoes or beetroot.)

Apple (and other fruit) Purées

4 lb (2 kg) cooking apples
4 oz (100 g) or more sugar to
   counteract extreme tartness

Turn freezer control to coldest setting.

Wash, finely peel, core and quarter apples. Simmer, just covered with water and a lid, until almost cooked, 15–20 mins. Add sugar and finish cooking. Leave as they are with juice; whizz to a purée in an electric blender with the blades well covered with some of the cooking juices, or drain, mash apple finely with a fork and re-mix with the cooking juice.

Cool, pack, freeze, store and thaw as for carrots, above.

(Apricots, fresh or dried, pears, prunes, plums or peaches can be frozen in this way. If preparation and cooking guidance is needed, see 'Purées Galore'.)

Minced Beef Casserole

2 lb (1 kg) lean stewing beef	4 tbsps vegetable oil
1 small onion for babies over	1 small can tomato purée
8 mths	½ teasp Marmite or yeast
3 carrots	extract for babies over 8 mths
2 parsnips	1 pint (500 ml) Baby Soup
1 small swede	Stock, page 116, or water

Turn freezer to coldest setting.

Make sure the meat is fat free and either ask your butcher to mince it finely for you specially, or do it yourself in a mincer or electric chopper. (Ready-minced beef from the butcher is too fat for babies unless you toss it in a non-stick frying pan over a medium to high heat, separating the pieces as you turn it, and drain off the fat as it runs off the meat. Continue until all fat is removed from meat in this way, then use in recipe as ready-minced lean meat.) Chop onion finely, if used. Wash, peel and slice or dice carrots, parsnips and swede.

Heat the oil in a large pan, toss the onion in it until soft, add the meat and stir gently until brown all over. Add the prepared carrots, parsnips and swede with the tomato purée, Marmite, if used, and enough stock or water to cover the meat and half the vegetables. Bring to the boil and simmer gently, covered, until meat and vegetables are cooked, 20–30 mins.

Cool quickly by standing pan in cold or iced water. Skim off any surface fat.

Pack in portion-sized containers – lidded plastic boxes, waxed or foil cartons – leaving ½ inch (1 cm) head space. Label with recipe name, date and storage life.

Freeze immediately, until solid, and return freezer control to normal.

Store up to 2 mths.

Thaw by dipping container into warm water to loosen the block and heat over simmering water in a basin or in the top of a double saucepan, bringing to the boil and stirring to prevent sticking if necessary.

For babies under 6 mths, put through a hand blender before serving.

For older babies, mash if necessary and serve with peas, green beans or cabbage.

Lamb Hotpot

2 lb (1 kg) lean boneless lamb
2 lamb's kidneys
1 onion for babies over 8 mths
¼ white cabbage (about 8 oz, 225 g or so)

1 oz (25 g) margarine
¼ teasp salt for babies over 8 mths
¼ pint (5 fl oz, 125 ml) Baby Soup Stock, page 116, or water

Turn freezer control to lowest setting.

Trim all fat from lamb and cut into small cubes. After removing fat, skin and hard core from kidneys, wash, dry and slice them. Chop the onion finely, if used. Trim off any blemished outer leaves, wash and shred cabbage. Melt the margarine in a large pan and toss the onion in it until soft. Add the meat and kidney and stir gently until brown all over. Add shredded cabbage, salt if used, and simmer, just covered with stock or water, and a lid, until meat is tender, 1 hr or more.

Cool, pack, freeze, store and thaw as for Minced Beef Casserole, above.

For babies under 6 mths, put through a hand blender.

For older babies, serve with mashed potatoes and carrots or a green vegetable.

Chicken with Celery

8–9 stalks celery	¼ teasp salt for babies over
1 medium chicken or small fowl	8 mths
2 oz (50 g) butter	

Turn the freezer control to coldest setting.

Wash and chop the celery. Joint the chicken with a sharp knife and cut the breast and other flesh neatly away from the carcass.

Melt the butter in a large pan and turn pieces of chicken in it until lightly brown all over. Drain away any excess butter. Cover chicken with celery and salt, if used, just cover chicken with water and simmer with lid on until chicken is tender, 25–35 mins, or 1 hr or more for a fowl. (The carcass can be used for Baby Soup Stock.)

Cool quickly by standing pan in cold or iced water. Skim off any excess fat.

Pack in portion-sized containers with the cooking liquid, leaving ½ inch (1 cm) head space and include leg and wing bones. Label with name, date and storage life.

Freeze immediately, until solid, and return freezer control to normal.

Store up to 3 mths.

Thaw by immersing container in warm water to release the block and heat over simmering water in a basin or in the top of a double saucepan until it reaches boiling point.

For babies under 6 mths, drain, remove flesh from the bones and put chicken and celery through a hand blender before mixing with enough of the cooking liquid to make a smooth purée. (Use the rest of the liquid as a soup or mixed with puréed vegetables.)

For an older baby, unless she has learned to cope with bones, drain, remove the flesh and dice or mash. Thicken the cooking liquid with 1 dessertsp or so of baby rice, reheat with the chicken and celery and serve with sprouts or peas and mashed potatoes.

Liver and Tomatoes

2 lb (1 kg) lamb's, calf's or ox
  liver
1 large tin tomatoes (1 lb 12 oz,
  792 g, size)

¼ teasp salt for babies over
  8 mths

Turn freezer control to coldest setting.

Wash and dry liver, cut away any skin, tubes or coarse connective tissue, and slice. Put the tomatoes and juice through a sieve, discarding skin and seeds.

Simmer sieved tomatoes and juice with the liver, and salt, if used, covered, until tender, 20–30 mins. Or bake, covered with foil, at 350°F (180°C), Gas 4, until tender, about 40 mins.

Cool, pack, freeze, store and thaw as for Minced Beef Casserole.

For babies under 6 mths, put through a hand blender.

For older babies, serve chopped with mashed potatoes and a green vegetable – spinach is very good with this.

Fish Stew

2 lb (1 kg) filleted fish (cod,
  coley, haddock, etc)
¼ teasp salt for babies over
  8 mths

1 lb (500 g) carrots
1 tin tomatoes (14 oz,
  396 g size)

Switch freezer control to coldest setting.

Prepare, steam with salt, if used, skin and check fish for stray bones, as in Fish Purée, page 42, but flake, do not purée.

Clean, peel and slice carrots. Sieve tomatoes and juice, discarding skin and seeds. While fish is cooking in the steamer, simmer the sliced carrots with the puréed tomatoes and juice in the pan below.

Combine cooked flaked fish with the tomatoes and carrots.

Cool, pack, freeze, store and thaw as for Minced Beef Casserole.

For babies under 6 mths, put through a hand blender.

Beef Loaf

1 lb (500 g) lean stewing beef	¼ teasp salt for babies over
2 oz (50 g) butter	8 mths
6 oz (150 g) brown breadcrumbs	½ pint (250 ml) Baby Soup
1 small onion, fine'y chopped,	Stock or water
for babies over 8 mths	
2 eggs, beaten – yolks only for	
babies under 8 mths	

Turn freezer control to coldest setting.

Make sure beef is fat free and ask your butcher to mince it finely for you; do it yourself in a mincer or electric chopper; or fry butcher's ready-minced meat in a non-stick frying pan as suggested in Minced Beef Casserole, page 120.

Grease a straight-sided baking tin (2 lb, 1 kg size) with butter and coat with 2 oz (50 g) breadcrumbs.

Melt the rest of the butter and soften onion in it, if used. Mix the meat, softened onion, breadcrumbs, beaten eggs, salt if used, and the stock to a very thick dropping consistency. Turn into the prepared tin, cover with foil and bake at 350°F (180°C), Gas 4, until cooked, about 1½ hrs.

Cool quickly by standing tin in cold or iced water.

Pack, after cutting into portion-sized pieces and wrapping individually in overlapping foil or in thick polythene bags, sealed with wire twists or small, plastic lidded boxes. Label with the name of the recipe, the date and the storage life.

Freeze immediately until solid, then return freezer control to normal.

Store up to 2 mths.

Thaw at room temperature for 4 hrs and reheat in covered baking dish at 350°F (180°C), Gas 4, for 20–30 mins, or until heated right through (as hot as if it had just been cooked). Or heat over simmering water in a basin or in the top of a double boiler with 2 or 3 tbsps water.

For babies under 6 mths, put through a hand blender and mix with boiled baby milk or water to obtain a smooth consistency.

For older babies, mash or chop for finger feeding, according to stage reached, and serve with skinned and de-seeded tomatoes and a green vegetable.

Further Suggestions

Most of your favourite baby recipes could be adapted for freezing on the lines of the foregoing recipes. Amongst those in various other sections of this book, the following are practical to make and freeze in larger amounts – just multiply the quantities given to suit your needs, and follow the instructions for cooking, packing, labelling, freezing, storing and thawing given in the 'Meals to Freeze' recipes.

From 'Nutritious Meat Dishes', pages 45–56

Taffy's Stew
Shepherd's Pie
Irish Stew
Chicken and Apricots
Veal Blanquette
Braised Brains and Broccoli

Kidney Special
Kidney and Beef Pâté
Liver Mash
Liver and Beef Pâté
Liver Casserole

From 'Ideas for Fish', pages 57–63

Haddock with Orange
Fish Mould

Mini Fish Cakes

From 'Simple Soups', pages 64–9

Small Stocks (1, 2, 3 or 4)
Vegetable Broth
Lentil Soup (add milk, if used, after freezing

Chicken and Celery Soup
Mini Minestrone (add cheese after freezing)

From 'Vegetable Variety', pages 78–84

Baby Bavarian Cabbage
Cauliflower Cheese
Celery and Tomato Cheese
Cheese Mix
Courgette with Tomato and Cheese

Eggy Carrot
Marrow Cheese
Potato Casserole
Vegetable Mould
Vegetable Timbale

From 'Scrumptious Puddings', pages 85–90

Apple Brown Betty
Fruit Jelly
Lemon Egg Jelly
Milk Jelly

Orange and Honey Bread Pudding
Rice Flummery

From 'Irresistible Ices', pages 91–6

all in this section

From 'Finger Foods and Teatime Titbits', pages 97–103

Sandwiches, if frozen when freshly made

Lemon Curd

From 'Meatless Baby Fare', pages 104–14

Black-eyed Bean Stew

Cauliflower and Lentils

Chick Pea Stew

Haricot Bean Stew

Lentil Cheese

Nut Roast

Red Bean Stew

Soya Bean Curd

Soya Bean Loaf

Soya Bean Stew

Vegetable Protein Loaf

Adapting Family Meals for a Baby

When a baby is eating with the family, it is often easier to share the same meal, adapting it to suit the needs of each.

Here are some family favourites that lend themselves to this, with very little extra trouble. It is mostly a question of taking out the baby's portion before adding any potentially upsetting ingredients.

Quantities are for two or three, as well as a baby, of up to twelve to eighteen months, after which you can expect her to eat more or less what the rest of the family is having.

Meat Dishes

Casserole of Beef

1 lb (500 g) braising beef
1 onion
8 oz (225 g) carrots
8 oz (225 g) parsnips
1 small swede
4–5 stalks celery
4 tbsps vegetable oil

¾ pint (15 fl oz, 375 ml) Baby
  Soup Stock, page 116, or water
salt and pepper
1 bay leaf
2 teasps chopped parsley
pinch thyme
3 tbsps flour

Trim any fat off the meat. Chop the onion finely. Clean, peel and slice the carrots, parsnips and swede. Clean and chop the celery.

Heat the oil, soften the onion and brown the meat lightly in it.

Remove from pan and pour away any remaining oil. Place vegetables in the bottom of the pan with the meat on top. Add enough stock or water to cover the vegetables. Cover and simmer slowly, or bake at 350°F (180°C), Gas 4, until the meat is tender, about 2 hrs.

Baby: Remove a piece of meat, a selection of vegetables and 3–4 tbsps of the liquid. Leave to cool, skim off any surplus fat, and put through a hand blender, mash or chop, according to stage reached.

Rest of family: Season casserole to taste, add bay leaf, parsley and thyme. Mix flour to a paste with a little water, stir into casserole and bring to the boil, stirring gently. Simmer for a further 15 mins.

(Lamb, chicken, veal, ham steaks, liver or any other meat or offal can be braised for the whole family in a similar way.)

Beef with Prunes

8 oz (225 g) prunes	4 tbsps vegetable oil
1–1½ lb (500–750 g) lean braising beef	½ pint (10 fl oz, 250 ml) Baby Soup Stock, page 116, or water
1 onion	salt and pepper
8 oz (225 g) carrots	3 tbsps flour

Soak prunes overnight, then prepare, cook and serve as for Casserole of Beef above, placing the carrots in the bottom of the pan with the prunes and browned meat on top.

Braised Stuffed Heart

For stuffing

4 oz (100 g) breadcrumbs
2 teasps chopped parsley
¼ teasp mixed herbs
salt and pepper

¼ teasp grated lemon rind
4 tbsps (2 oz, 50 g) margarine
½ egg
milk or water

4 lambs' or sheep's hearts
2 onions
nut of margarine

½ pint (10 fl oz, 250 ml) Baby
 Soup Stock (page 116), or
 water

First make stuffing. Mix breadcrumbs, parsley, herbs, seasoning and lemon rind, add melted margarine and egg with enough milk or water to give a stiff consistency that will hold together.

Trim all fat, gristle and blood vessels from the hearts, then wash under running water before soaking them in cold water to remove all the blood. Drain and wipe hearts dry on absorbent kitchen paper. With scissors, extend the division at the top of the heart to make a cavity in three of the hearts. Fill each with the stuffing, and sew up the top of the hearts with white cotton.

Chop the onions finely. Heat the nut of margarine in a pan, brown the stuffed hearts all over in it, then in the same fat, lightly sauté the onions and put on one side with the hearts. Pour away any remaining fat, return the onions and the hearts, adding the unstuffed heart, to the pan with stock or water half-way up hearts. Simmer slowly, covered, until tender, about 1½ hrs.

Baby : Remove the unstuffed heart with 1–2 tbsps cooking liquid. Leave liquid to cool while you chop or put heart through a blender, according to stage reached, skim fat off liquid and add liquid to heart.

Rest of family : Add seasoning to taste and serve stuffed hearts with onions and some of the cooking liquid.

Both : Serve with mashed potatoes and a green vegetable.

Creamed Sweetbreads

4 sweetbreads	½ teasp or so baby cereal
4 carrots	

For sauce

2 tbsps butter	½ teasp thyme
1 large onion, grated	3 tbsps chopped parsley
2 tbsps flour	3 dessertsps lemon juice
½ pint (10 fl oz, 250 ml) milk	salt and pepper
1 bay leaf	4 tbsps sherry (optional)

Soak sweetbreads (calves' or sheep's) in cold water for 1 hr to remove blood, strain and simmer, covered with water, for 10 mins. Drain, and cool sweetbreads in cold water before removing skin and coarse fibres. Clean, peel and slice carrots and simmer with sweetbreads, just covered with water, and a lid, until tender, about 1 hr.

Meantime make a sauce. Heat butter, sauté onion in it until soft, stir in flour, add milk slowly, then add bay leaf, thyme, parsley, lemon juice, salt and pepper. Stir over a low heat until the sauce boils, then simmer slowly, covered, for a further 3 mins.

Baby: Remove a small portion of cooked sweetbreads and carrots with a little of the cooking liquid. Blend or chop sweetbreads according to stage reached. Mix with mashed or chopped carrot, the cooking liquid and ½ teasp baby cereal, or enough to make a creamy sauce.

Rest of family: Combine the white sauce with the sweetbreads, sherry, if used, and some of the cooking liquid and simmer, half covered, for a further 10 mins.

Both: Serve with potatoes and peas.

Family Stew

1 lb (500 g) lean boneless meat	1 bay leaf
1 lb (500 g) mixed vegetables	3 teasps chopped parsley
¾ pint (15 fl oz, 375 ml) Baby Soup Stock, page 116, or water	½ teasp marjoram, thyme or oregano
1 teasp salt	3 tbsps flour
¼ teasp pepper	

Cut meat in cubes (beef, lamb, veal, rabbit, chicken or fowl are all suitable). Wash, peel and slice vegetables (predominantly carrots, with some swede, parsnip and celery is a good mixture).

Simmer meat and vegetables, just covered with stock or water, and a lid, slowly, until the meat is tender, 1–2 hrs.

Baby: Remove a portion of meat, vegetables and cooking liquid, and leave to cool. Skim off any surplus fat. Put through a hand blender, mash or chop according to the stage reached, and mix with the cooking liquid.

Rest of family: Add salt, pepper, bay leaf, parsley and other herbs to stew. Make a smooth paste with the flour and a little of the cooking liquid. Stir this into stew, bring back to the boil, stirring, and simmer slowly for a further 15 mins.

Both: Serve with mashed potatoes and peas or green beans.

Kidneys in Tomato Sauce

¼ lb (100 g) macaroni	2 teasps chopped parsley or chives
7 lambs' kidneys	1 teasp basil
4 oz (100 g) lean ham	salt and pepper
1 pint (20 fl oz, 500 ml) Baby Soup Stock, page 116, or water	2 tbsps cornflour
8 tbsps thick tomato purée, page 35	

Cook macaroni according to pack instructions and keep warm. Remove fat, skin and tubes from kidneys, wash well and slice.

Dice ham and simmer with sliced kidneys, stock or water, covered, until tender, 5–10 mins.

Baby: Remove slices equivalent to about 1 kidney and put through a hand blender, with 1–2 tbsps cooked macaroni, or chop, according to stage reached. Mix kidney and macaroni with 2 tbsps tomato purée.

Rest of family: Add parsley or chives, basil, the rest of the tomato purée and seasoning to taste, to the stew. Blend the cornflour with a little cold water, add to stew, stirring, until the mixture thickens and boils. Simmer for a further 3 mins.

Serve kidneys and sauce surrounded by macaroni and accompanied by a green vegetable.

Liver Pâté

8 oz (225 g) lamb's or ox liver	½ teasp grated onion
½ teasp gelatine	1 teasp Worcestershire sauce
6 fl oz (150 ml) water	salt and pepper

Wash liver, cut away any skin, tubes or connective tissue, and simmer, with the water, covered by a lid, until cooked, 7–10 mins.

Dissolve the gelatine by stirring into the hot liver and cooking liquid. Pour into an electric liquidizer and whizz until smooth.

Baby: Take out a small portion. For those under 6 mths, serve as it is or chill in the refrigerator in a mould and blend with a little baby milk to obtain the right consistency. For older babies, unmould, and serve sliced or diced with tomatoes, skinned and de-seeded.

Rest of family: Add onion, Worcestershire sauce, salt and pepper to taste and blend liver for a few secs more. Turn into a mould, cool, and refrigerate.

Serve sliced with salad, or with toast as an hors d'oeuvre.

Meat Loaf

1 lb (500 g) lean stewing or braising meat	$\frac{1}{4}$ teasp ground mace
	$\frac{1}{4}$ teasp mixed herbs
4 heaped tbsps brown breadcrumbs	1 small clove garlic (optional)
	1 teasp salt
1 tbsp grated onion	$\frac{1}{4}$ teasp pepper

Mince meat finely in a mincer or electric chopper, or ask your butcher to do it for you. (Ready-minced butcher's beef is not suitable for a baby unless you prepare it as suggested in Minced Beef Casserole, page 120.) Mix the meat with the breadcrumbs.

Baby: Take out a small portion, shape into a loaf and wrap in foil. Bake on a heatproof dish at 350°F (180°C), Gas 4, or steam, for 1 hr. Put through a hand blender and mix with a little baby milk or water, or dice, according to stage reached, and serve with tomato purée, page 35.

Rest of family: Add the onion, mace, mixed herbs, garlic, crushed, if used, salt and pepper to the meat mixture. Pack into a greased tin, cover with foil, and bake at 350°F (180°C), Gas 4, or steam for 1–1$\frac{1}{2}$ hrs, until the meat is tender.

If you have time, serve with a tomato sauce made as follows: fry an onion, finely chopped, in 3 tbsps vegetable oil until soft, stirring in 3 tbsps flour, then slowly, $\frac{1}{2}$ pint (250 ml) tomato juice and $\frac{1}{2}$ pint (250 ml) stock or water. Add a bay leaf, $\frac{1}{2}$ teasp sugar, salt and pepper to taste, bring to the boil, stirring, and simmer for $\frac{1}{2}$ hr. Strain before pouring sauce over hot meat loaf prior to serving hot with mashed potatoes.

Or serve cold, sliced, with salad.

Meat Jellies

12 oz (350 g) freshly cooked lean meat (no salt)	squeeze lemon juice
1½ level tbsps gelatine	salt and pepper
¾ pint (15 fl oz, 375 ml) Baby Soup Stock, page 116, or water	3 tbsps sherry (optional)
	½ clove garlic finely crushed (optional)

Make sure all skin, fat and gristle are removed from cooked meat (beef, lamb, ham, veal, chicken, turkey or a mixture of these are suitable). Mince meat finely in a mincer, electric chopper, grinder, put through a hand blender, or chop very small.

Dissolve gelatine in 5 tbsps stock or water, stirring over gentle heat. Add rest of stock and chill by standing in cold or iced water. Before it begins to set, stir in minced, cooked meat.

Baby: Put a portion in a small mould and refrigerate until set, 1 hr or so. Put through a hand blender or dice or slice according to stage reached and serve with any puréed or diced vegetable.

Rest of family: To the meat jelly mixture, add lemon juice, seasoning to taste, sherry and garlic, if used, and stir well. Pour into one or several individual moulds. Refrigerate to set, 3–4 hrs. Serve sliced with salad.

Roast Meat

Roast beef, lamb, chicken, turkey, veal or very lean pork with no seasoning or strong flavourings, and covered with a lid or foil, or in a roast bag, to avoid basting with fat.

Baby: When meat is cooked, carve a small, lean portion and draw 2–3 tbsps liquid from the meat by pressing a spoon into the joint. Leave liquid to cool while you put the meat for baby through a hand blender or chop it. Skim fat off meat juices, then mix juice with meat.

Rest of family: Add seasoning and other flavourings to taste, baste meat well with the juices and fats that have collected round the meat and continue to cook, uncovered, for a further 10–15 mins at a lower heat.

Both : Serve with potatoes (mashed or baked in their jackets for baby, not roasted) and vegetables.

Tripe (and Onions)

1 lb (500 g) dressed tripe   baby cereal
juice of ½ lemon

For sauce

3 tbsps butter   ¼ pint (5 fl oz, 125 ml) milk
2 tbsps flour   salt and pepper
2 onions sliced

Wash tripe, cut into pieces, cover with cold water, bring to the boil and simmer for 2 mins. Drain, just cover tripe with fresh cold water, add the lemon juice and simmer, covered, until tender, about 1 hr.

Baby : Remove a small portion of cooked tripe and 2–3 tbsps cooking liquid. Put tripe through a hand blender or chop. Mix the cooking liquid with enough baby cereal to make a thickish sauce and heat thoroughly with the tripe before serving.

Rest of family : Make a sauce with the butter, onions, flour, seasoning, milk and liquid in which tripe has cooked, as in Creamed Sweetbreads, page 131. Stir in tripe, heat thoroughly and serve.

Fish for All

Baked Fish

4 fillets or steaks white fish   2 tbsps lemon juice
1 dessertsp butter

For sauce

3 tbsps margarine   pinch nutmeg
3 tbsps flour   salt and pepper
1 pint (20 fl oz, 500 ml)   6 tbsps grated Cheddar cheese
   vegetable stock or water

Wash and dry fish (cod, halibut, coley, haddock, plaice, sole or other white fish, fresh or frozen). Fold thin fillets like sole and plaice in half.

Baby : Smear one small fillet or steak lightly with butter, add a dash of salt for those over 8 mths, wrap in cooking foil and place on a heatproof dish. Bake at 350°F (180°C), Gas 4, until flakes separate easily, 20–30 mins. Remove any skin and bones from fish, mash, put through a hand blender, or flake, according to stage reached, adding a little heated milk to give a smoother consistency if necessary.

Rest of family : Place fish in a shallow baking dish. Melt butter, add lemon juice, pour over fish and cover with a lid or foil. Bake at 350°F (180°C), Gas 4, for 20–30 mins. Meantime make a cheese sauce: melt margarine in a pan, stir in flour and vegetable stock, slowly. Add nutmeg, salt and pepper to taste, and simmer for 3 mins. Just before removing from heat, stir in cheese, but do not re-boil.

Serve fish with cheese sauce poured over it, accompanied by mashed potatoes (duchesse-style go very well) and a green vegetable.

Creamed Soft Roes

8 soft herring roes
¼ pint (5 fl oz, 125 ml) milk
1½ tbsps flour
few drops lemon juice

salt and pepper
3 slices toast
½ teasp chopped parsley

Wash roes and simmer gently in the milk, covered, until tender, 10–15 mins. Remove with a draining spoon, and put liquid on one side.

Baby : Take one herring roe (or more according to appetite), put through blender or chop and serve mixed with a little of the milky cooking liquid.

Rest of family : Mix flour to a paste with a little cold water, add milk in which roes have cooked, return to pan, stir until it boils and simmer for 3 mins. Add lemon juice, salt and pepper to taste.

Serve roes on toast, covered with sauce and garnished with parsley.

Fish Cakes

8 oz (225 g) freshly cooked, mashed potatoes
8 oz (225 g) freshly cooked, filleted cod, coley or other white fish
1 egg, beaten
1 teasp salt

¼ teasp pepper
pinch nutmeg
1 tbsp chopped parsley
few drops lemon juice
oil for frying
4 tbsps crushed cornflakes

Baby : Take a portion of the fish and potato. Remove fish skin, check carefully for stray bones and put through a hand blender. Mash fish and potato together with a little baby milk to make a smooth purée for babies up to 6 mths.

Rest of family : Mix all ingredients, except oil and crushed cornflakes, form into cakes, coat with crushed cornflakes and fry in hot oil, browning each side and cooking right through.

Poached Creamed Fish

4 fillets or frozen bricks white fish	¼ pint (5 fl oz, 125 ml) milk ¼ pint (5 fl oz, 125 ml) water

For sauce

1 tbsp butter	½ tbsp vinegar
2 tbsps flour	1 teasp salt
½ bay leaf	a sprinkle of black pepper
2 teasps chopped parsley	

Wash and dry fish and simmer with the milk and water, just below boiling, until flakes separate easily. Lift fish out with a fish slice and strain cooking liquid before putting on one side.

Baby: Take a small fillet or steak of the fish, remove any skin and check carefully for bones before putting through a hand blender, mashing, or chopping. Mix with a little of the strained cooking liquid to make a smooth purée.

Rest of family: Using the cooking liquid, strained, make a roux sauce: melt butter, stir in flour, add liquid slowly, then the bay leaf, parsley, vinegar and seasoning to taste. Heat the fish in the sauce for 1 min.

Both: Serve with potatoes and spinach, or another green vegetable.

Cheese and Eggs

Cheese Pudding

5 oz (125 g) grated Cheddar cheese	1 tbsp vegetable oil salt and pepper
3 oz (75 g) breadcrumbs	½ teasp mixed herbs
3 eggs	½ teasp mixed mustard
¾ pint (15 fl oz, 375 ml) milk	1 dessertsp chopped parsley
1 oz (25 g) butter	

Put 4 oz (100 g) cheese, all the breadcrumbs, beaten eggs (yolks only at this stage if baby is under 8 mths), in a bowl, and mix well. Bring milk and butter to the boil and pour over the bread-crumbs. Mix.

Baby: Spoon a portion into a lightly oiled casserole and bake at 350°F (180°C), Gas, 4, or steam, for 30 mins. Put through a hand blender, if under 6 mths, and mix with a little boiled water to give a smooth consistency.

Rest of family: Add egg whites, beaten, if not included already, along with salt and pepper to taste, herbs and mustard. Pour into an oiled pie dish, sprinkle rest of cheese on top and bake at 350°F (180°C), Gas 4, or steam, until firm, about 30–40 mins. Garnish with parsley before serving.

Cheese and Tomato Risotto

1 tin tomatoes (14 oz, 396 g size)
½ pint (250 ml) water
8 oz (225 g) long-grain rice
6 oz (150 g) grated Cheddar cheese
1 clove garlic, finely crushed
¼ teasp basil
salt and pepper

Sieve tomatoes, discarding seeds and skins. Bring water, sieved tomatoes and juice to the boil, add rice and simmer slowly, covered, for 13 mins. Stir in grated cheese until it melts.

Baby: Remove a small portion and put through a hand blender for those under 6 mths.

Rest of family: Add crushed garlic, basil, salt and pepper to taste and stir risotto over a low heat for 1 min, adding a little water if it is too dry.

Serve with a crisp salad of chopped white cabbage, apple and nuts.

Eggs Florentine

12 oz (350 g) fresh or frozen spinach	4 eggs
	salt and pepper
6 oz (150 g) grated Cheddar cheese	small nut butter

Wash fresh spinach in several changes of cold water to remove all grit, cut off stalk, then put into ½ inch (1 cm) boiling water and simmer until tender, 15–20 mins. Cook frozen spinach according to pack instructions. Drain well, return to pan, and stir in two thirds of the cheese until it melts. Either hard-boil or poach the eggs.

Baby: If under 8 mths, take a portion of spinach and an egg yolk and put through a hand blender. For older babies, chop egg and serve on a bed of chopped or blended spinach.

Rest of family: Season spinach and cheese to taste, turn into a shallow heatproof dish, lay cooked eggs on top, sprinkle with remaining grated cheese, dot with butter. Grill until cheese melts.

Lentil and Cheese Soup

8 oz (225 g) lentils	4 oz (100 g) grated Cheddar cheese
1 carrot, diced	
1 onion, sliced	pinch dried thyme
1 turnip, diced	pinch basil
2 pints (1 litre) Baby Soup Stock (page 116), or water	1 teasp salt or to taste
	a sprinkle of black pepper
3 tbsps baby milk	¼ pint (5 fl oz, 125 ml) milk

Wash lentils and simmer with the prepared vegetables in the stock or water until lentils are very soft, ¾–1 hr. Drain off liquid and put on one side. Mash lentils and vegetables, or put through a sieve, or whizz in an electric blender with some of the liquid, and then return to the rest of the liquid.

Baby: Take out a portion, 5 or 6 tbsps or more, add the baby milk, bring to the boil, stir in ¼ of the cheese (1 oz, 25 g) but do not re-boil, and serve with wholemeal bread rusks.

Rest of family : Reheat the soup, adding herbs, salt and pepper to taste, and simmer for a further 10 mins. Add milk and cheese, continuing to heat, but remove before it boils. Serve with croutons of fried or toasted bread.

Quiche

For pastry

6 oz (150 g) flour   3 oz (75 g) fat

For filling

½ oz (12 g) butter   few drops vegetable oil
1 tbsp grated onion   1 teasp salt
3 eggs   ½ teasp prepared mustard
½ pint (10 fl oz, 250 ml) milk   few drops Worcestershire sauce
8 oz (225 g) grated Cheddar   pinch paprika
  cheese   a sprinkle of black pepper

Make pastry and line a 7 inch (18 cm approx) flan tin. Bake blind at 450°F (230°C), Gas 8, for 15–20 mins.

Melt butter and cook onion in it until soft. Blend eggs lightly, stir in milk and grated cheese.

Baby : Put 5–6 tbsps of the egg, milk and cheese mixture into a lightly oiled casserole. Bake at 350°F (180°C), Gas 4, with filled family flan until set, about 20 mins. Serve with peeled, de-seeded tomatoes.

Rest of family : Add remaining ingredients to the egg, cheese and milk mixture and pour into pre-cooked pastry case. Bake at 350°F (180°C), Gas 4, until set, 30–40 mins, covering pastry with foil if it is likely to burn.

Serve garnished with a ring of sliced tomatoes and accompanied by a salad.

Vegetable and Cheese Casserole

3 tbsps vegetable oil
1 onion, finely chopped
3 carrots, sliced
2 parsnips, sliced
3 turnips, sliced
1 swede, sliced
6 oz (150 g) grated cheese

1 large tin tomatoes (1 lb 12 oz, 792 g size)
8 tbsps brown breadcrumbs
salt and pepper
1 teasp mixed herbs
½ teasp basil
dot butter

Heat oil and soften onion in it. Lightly oil both a baby-sized and a family-sized casserole.

Baby : Fill casserole with layers of vegetables, excluding the onion, sprinkling each layer with cheese (use about 1½ oz, 40 g). Sieve 1 or 2 of the tinned tomatoes, mix with 3–4 tbsps of the tomato juice, and pour over the layered vegetables.

Sprinkle the top with grated cheese and breadcrumbs, cover with foil and bake at 350°F (180°C), Gas 4, until all the vegetables are tender, about 1 hr. Put through a hand blender, mash or chop to suit your baby.

Rest of family : Fill casserole as for baby, but include softened onion and add seasoning and a sprinkling of herbs between each layer of vegetables. Chop tinned tomatoes roughly and pour with juice over casserole before sprinkling the top with cheese and breadcrumbs. Dot with butter and bake at 350°F (180°C), Gas 4, for 1 hr or more until all vegetables are tender.

Cheese Cake

For case

8 oz (225 g) digestive biscuits   4 oz (100 g) melted butter

For filling

2 eggs   ½ teasp vanilla essence
2 tbsps sugar   2 teasps lemon juice
8 oz (225 g) curd cheese

Crush or whizz biscuits in an electric blender, then mix well with melted butter, and press flat onto the base of a cake tin.

Whizz the eggs, sugar and curd cheese in an electric blender; or whisk the eggs and mix well with cheese and sugar with a wooden spoon.

Baby: Remove a portion of the cheese mixture, 4–5 tbsps, and put into a small buttered casserole. Bake with the family cheese cake at 325°F (160°C), Gas 3, until set, about 20 mins.

Rest of family: Add vanilla essence and lemon juice to cheese mixture, turn onto prepared biscuit base. Bake at 325°F (160°C), Gas 3, until set, about 30 mins. (This makes a good pudding with fresh fruit.)

Index to Recipes

Index to Recipes

Notes

Notes

Notes